Confessions of a
Black Magician

Some Other Titles from The Original Falcon Press

Christopher S. Hyatt, Ph.D.
   Undoing Yourself With Energized Meditation & Other Devices
   Techniques for Undoing Yourself (CDs)
   Radical Undoing: Complete Course for Undoing Yourself (DVDs & CDs)
   Energized Hypnosis (book, CDs & DVDs)
   To Lie Is Human: Not Getting Caught Is Divine
   Secrets of Western Tantra: The Sexuality of the Middle Path

Christopher S. Hyatt, Ph.D. with contributions by
Wm. S. Burroughs, Timothy Leary, Robert Anton Wilson et al.
   Rebels & Devils: The Psychology of Liberation

Christopher S. Hyatt, Ph.D. & Antero Alli
   A Modern Shaman's Guide to a Pregnant Universe

S. Jason Black and Christopher S. Hyatt, Ph.D.
   Pacts With the Devil: A Chronicle of Sex, Blasphemy & Liberation
   Urban Voodoo: A Beginner's Guide to Afro-Caribbean Magic

Antero Alli
   Angel Tech: A Modern Shaman's Guide to Reality Selection
   Angel Tech Talk (CDs)

Peter J. Carroll
   The Chaos Magick Audio CDs
   PsyberMagick

Phil Hine
   Condensed Chaos: An Introduction to Chaos Magic
   Prime Chaos: Adventures in Chaos Magic
   The Pseudonomicon

Joseph Lisiewski, Ph.D.
   Israel Regardie and the Philosopher's Stone
   Ceremonial Magic and the Power of Evocation
   Kabbalistic Cycles and the Mastery of Life
   Kabbalistic Handbook for the Practicing Magician
   Howlings from the Pit

Israel Regardie
   The Complete Golden Dawn System of Magic
   What You Should Know About the Golden Dawn
   The Golden Dawn Audio CDs

Stephen Sennitt
   The Infernal Texts: NOX & Liber Koth

For up-to-the-minute information on prices and availability, please visit our website at http://originalfalcon.com

CONFESSIONS OF A BLACK MAGICIAN

by
Nathan Neuharth

THE *Original* FALCON PRESS
TEMPE, ARIZONA, U.S.A.

Copyright © 2010 by Nathan Neuharth

All rights reserved. No part of this book, in part or in whole, may be reproduced, transmitted, or utilized, in any form or by any means, electronic or mechanical, including photocopying, recording, or by any information storage and retrieval system, without permission in writing from the publisher, except for brief quotations in critical articles, books and reviews.

International Standard Book Number: 978-1-935150-79-4
Library of Congress Catalog Card Number: 2010938750

First Edition 2010

Cover by P. Emerson Williams

The paper used in this publication meets the minimum requirements of the American National Standard for Permanence of Paper for Printed Library Materials Z39.48-1984

Address all inquiries to:
THE ORIGINAL FALCON PRESS
1753 East Broadway Road #101-277
Tempe, AZ 85282 U.S.A.
(or)
PO Box 3540
Silver Springs NV 89429 U.S.A.
**website: http://www.originalfalcon.com
email: info@originalfalcon.com**

You will not understand this…

Table of Contents

Part One
 The Birth of a Magician 9

Part Two
 The Babalon Isis Working 41

Part Three
 The Black Odyssey 93

Part Four
 Rosa Virgo 171

About the Author 192

Part One

The Birth of a Magician

"The only people for me are the mad ones, the ones who are mad to live, mad to talk, mad to be saved, desirous of everything at the same time, the ones who never yawn or say a common place thing, but burn, burn, burn like fabulous yellow roman candles exploding like spiders across the stars..." — Jack Kerouac, *On the Road*

A few years ago I saw a movie called *The Last Time I Committed Suicide*. The story was inspired by a letter Neal Cassady wrote to his friend, Jack Kerouac. The title describes the last time Neal had things going really good and how he fucked it up and lost it all.

I can not count the number of times I've committed suicide.

And I'm still alive.

My eyes are wide open and all I see is darkness. A black hoodwink over the top of my head, I'm naked beneath a thin black robe and wearing bright red socks.

All around me I can sense wisps of movement, the shuffling of feet. Unfamiliar voices of men and women chant, pray, and declare in somber, confident tones rising and falling from whispers to shouts and back again. Their voices vibrate. I recognize some of the languages spoken besides English there is Hebrew, Latin, Enochian, and Greek.

"Bring him to me," a male voice commands.

A strong, firm hand grips my arm and guides me forward.

The voice addresses me. "You stand at the gateway of hidden knowledge between the Pillars of Joachim and Boaz. Know that to enter is to change. Do you will to enter?"

"I will it."

"Inheritor of a dying world, why do you seek to enter our sacred Temple? Why do you seek admission into our sacred Order?"

"I've wandered in darkness all my life. I seek the light. I believe the light to be found within this Order."

I reflexively let out a tiny gasp as the hoodwink is ripped away from my head. The room is dimly lit, but enough that my eyes take a moment to adjust to the light after coming from the utter blackness of the cloth. Candles of various colors flicker around the room. I stand between two large pillars, one black and one white, both covered in ancient Egyptian hieroglyphs telling at least one story I recognize. The story of the lovers Isis and Osiris and the betrayal of their brother Set. Set kills Osiris and scatters his remains. Isis and her son, Horus, gather Osiris' remains and resurrect him.

With me between the pillars is a large black altar made of two black cubes, one set on top of the other. Upon the altar rests a single red rose, a glass of red wine, burning incense, a small plate with bread and salt on it, a gold cross, and a burning red lamp.

Gathered like soldiers around the altar, pillars, and I are a dozen men and women dressed in black robes similar to mine and wearing matching red socks. Some of them have arcane symbols attached to their robes like military badges and honors. They all wear Egyptian headdress. Except for the man over seeing the initiation ritual, the Hierophant or High Priest, he sits in a throne east of the altar wearing a head piece that reminds me of the Catholic Pope. He is the only one in the room dressed in a white robe. The High Priest has a thin moustache and goatee and wields a long wooden staff notched with strange sigils and glyphs.

Standing directly in front of me is the big man who held my arm and stripped my hoodwink. Now he stands expressionless, breathing heavy, wielding a long, slender, silver sword, with its sharp tip to my neck. He's a large man, maybe 300 pounds, and over six feet tall. For some reason he doesn't wear a head dress. His head looks to have been shaved clean with a straight edge razor. His eyes are round and unblinking. A single bead of sweat hangs onto his left temple. In a deep, gruff voice, "In the name of the Morning and Evening Star we consecrate you in fire and purify you in water."

Two women approach, a blonde sprinkling water around me, and the other waving an incense stick in triangular patterns. One is blonde, the other brunette.

The High Priest speaks, "Thrice you will be slain for breaking this oath of secrecy to our Order. Your heart will be cut out, your throat will be slit, and your body will be burned. Do you wish to continue and be forever bound by this oath and this Order?"

"I do."

The big, bald man lowers the sword and walks away from me. The brunette whispers to me, "Kneel." I do as she says.

The High Priest continues, "Inheritor of a dying world. What is your name?"

"Parsifal du Lac."

"Long have you dwelt in darkness, Frater Parsifal du Lac, we receive you into our Order. Arise. Rise neophyte and knight, Parsifal du Lac."

I am Neophyte $0° = 0^\square$ of the Order of the Golden Dawn of the Temple of Isis.

After my initiation ritual is complete we gather in the dining room for a dinner. The ritual itself lasted an hour and a half. It started with me sitting alone in a room wearing my black robe for the first time (officially), staring at a single white candle's flame, flickering, meditating on that tiny burning light, listening to the chanting in the temple below. I had never met any of the members of the Order of the Golden Dawn before this day. When I arrived in the early afternoon there were very brief introductions and then we got straight down to business.

Now in the dining room we are gathered around a large polished dark wood table. Including myself, there are thirteen members present. The Order of the Golden Dawn is an international society with secrets that has existed in one form or another since the original Hermetic Order of the Golden Dawn was disband in the very beginning of the twentieth century.

On the table for dinner there are dinner rolls and crackers of all sorts and sizes, cheeses, carrots, celery, broccoli, cauliflower, pickles, radishes, sliced ham, turkey, and salami. In the center of the table is a fabulous cheesecake with red letters written in strawberry topping, 'Congratulations Frater Parsifal'.

Besides myself the other twelve members present are:

The High Priest, Frater Judah. He seems to be the man in charge or at least appears to believe he is the man in charge. He has a well kept moustache and goatee with long hair, reaching down just past his shoulders and talks like a used car salesman, a computer programmer by trade. I don't trust him at all. He's discussing the differences between Masonic rites and Golden Dawn rituals with Frater Dumas and Frater Abraham.

Frater Abraham seems to be the one who is really in charge. He is a thin man with black hair, charismatic, homosexual, a college professor. A professor of philosophy at a local university. He also runs a small business as a classical astrologer, making birth charts and advising people. He smiles often and seems very tactful. When Judah speaks there is a slyness in Abraham's eyes, a slyness that knows Judah is an attention seeking buffoon.

Frater Azazel is a therapist who specializes in working with institutionalized schizophrenics. He has a full beard and long brown hair. Very tall, lanky, and wiry. He is often dressed in black and always carries a holy bible. King James version. He likes to drink beer and smoke the occasional bit of marijuana.

Frater Alpha is the strangest of the group. Clean shaven with black hair showing the first signs of gray. He looks like anyone's neighbor at first glance, but strike up a conversation and he spins off into unexpected territories of the mind and cosmos. Today he is discussing nanotechnology with Frater Azazel.

Soror Amore Delamore is Frater Judah's blond girlfriend. She seems genuine and polite. Her skin is very pale with acne scars on her cheeks left from youth. She is very plain looking. I find it confusing. One moment I look at her and find myself slightly attracted to her. The next I find myself completely not attracted to her. She works for an airline company and sits quietly, absorbed in Frater Judah's Masonic talk at the dinner table.

Frater Dumas. Fat. Bald. Tall. Thick. Round. The man who held the sword to my neck. Listening in on everyone's conversations, I learn that Dumas is also a Mason. He seems to have a chip on his shoulder. He is the only one here who has not introduced himself to me in a friendly manner. He has not even said hi or acknowledged my presence since the initiation ritual ended. When he looks at me with those large blue eyes I feel an inner heat and hate. He seems to be jealous of me maybe.

Frater Lux is a very sweet guy. The youngest person here, in his early twenties. He is a plumber and declares himself a recovering alcoholic and active member of Alcoholics Anonymous. His arms are covered in colorful tattoos of Chinese dragons and biker skulls. Very soft spoken. Black rimmed glasses. Looks like he should be in a rock band.

Soror Titania is loud-mouthed, crass, cocky, sarcastic, absolutely intelligent and absolutely beautiful. She is a Puerto Rican spitfire and an artist specializing in oil paintings. She loves to argue and debate everything. Married with children.

Soror Lucid has long, black, curly hair, easily reaching her waist. She is soft spoken, a mother, and a wife. She decorates homes for a living. A very peaceful and loving woman. I notice her brown eyes lingering on my blue eyes more than once at the dinner table.

Frater Sothis is an old Italian. From what I've gathered his family, especially his father and grandfather, who are both dead now, were deeply involved in the mafia. Seems kind of strange to me, like you would only actually meet someone from the mafia in a Hollywood movie. Apparently after the death of his father, by gunshot to the head, he completely turned his back on organized crime and spends all his time investigating UFO sightings, alien abductions, crop circles, cattle mutilations, and similar endeavors. He rides a black Harley Davidson motorcycle, I noticed it parked outside when my wife and friends dropped me off.

Frater Gilgamesh works for a credit card company, very high up on the financial food chain. He has awkward mannerisms, tall, thin, graying hair, thick glasses, very professional, but lacking in social skills. He's a number cruncher and excels in sacred geometry and Kabbalah. A few years ago he went through a divorce and has been living in his mother's basement every since. His ex-wife moved out of state with his children.

Soror 139, besides being a member of the Order of the Golden Dawn, is a practicing Wiccan priestess and an active member of Alcoholics Anonymous. She and her husband, who is not present, run a farm together growing organic vegetables. In her mid-forties and very talkative, she often talks about her husband with a loving glow.

"So Parsifal tell us about yourself. What are your magickal beliefs? Interests?" Judah asks me now that the Masonic discussion has sputtered out.

I sense Dumas eyeing me, everyone is, they're curious to explore their newest initiate, but Dumas has daggers in his eyes aimed at me. I try to ignore him. His size is intimidating. I answer Judah's inquiry, "I am, of course, fond of the Golden Dawn tradition and western occultism. Other systems I'm pretty familiar with are shamanism and Chaos Magick."

"Shamanism?" Abraham smiles, "that's interesting. Tell us more about that."

"Mm, not much to tell really. Been exposed to it most of my life. I'm working under a medicine man right now. A dog soldier. He's a very good guy. Mostly I help him with ceremonies. Pipe ceremonies. Sweat lodge. Learning what I can."

Gilgamesh pipes in, "If you have found a real medicine man to work with, you are indeed a lucky man. I've been exploring Native American spirituality for a few years now. Mostly Hopi and Navajo. Which tribe is your medicine man from?"

"A Sioux tribe. I'm a Sioux as well."

"Strong people," Gilgamesh nods, "you don't look Native American."

"I know."

"What's Chaos Magick?" Lux asks, using his index finger to push his glasses back up his nose, "Sounds dark."

"Chaos magick is basically the deconstruction of magickal processes such as a ritual. The idea is to break it down and use what is essential and effective without the extra baggage. It's basically the idea that the belief system is the tool to work with. What you believe is not as important as the outcome. The belief is a means to an end."

"I've never heard of it. Fascinating." Lux takes a bite of a ham and cheese roll.

I continue, "Peter Carroll is a good author on the subject of Chaos Magick. He got it going, sorta, back in the old days. Seventies and eighties. Phil Hine is a good chaos magician, too. But I guess the real old school chaos magician is Austin Osman Spare."

"I don't know any of them," Lux says with a mouthful of food.

"I've read Pete Carroll," Judah says. "It's very interesting."

Everything is interesting, I think.

"I know of Spare's work," Abraham smiles. "He was a very talented artist. Vivid paintings. They are truly alive. Lost out to alcoholism in the end, from what I understood. He started in the Golden Dawn didn't he?"

"I can't remember," I answer. "If it wasn't the Hermetic Order of the Golden Dawn itself, it was one of the spinoff orders. I think he was in the A∴A∴ with Crowley for a short time. I have read that he struggled with drinking."

A tender voice. "How did you become interested in the western tradition? The Golden Dawn?" Soror Lucid asks, her innocent, big brown eyes drinking me in.

"Oh," I take a sip of cherry soda, "I suppose like a lot of people, I guess. Actually, I'm not sure how people get into magick. Just kind of happens, doesn't it? I tend to think, like the old tribal shaman, the magician doesn't choose to become a magician, but is chosen."

"You chose to be chosen," Alpha gives a grin.

"Okay," I nod, "I discovered Aleister Crowley when I was a teenager. Discovered him through rock and roll. Reading about Jimmy Page from *Led Zeppelin*, David Bowie, and Ozzy Osbourne's song *Mr. Crowley*. That's how I first heard of Crowley and his picture on *the Beatles* 'Sgt. Pepper's Lonely Hearts Club Band' album cover. The first book I tried to read was *Confessions of Aleister Crowley*. It was too much for me at the time. But it was through Crowley that I discovered the Golden Dawn."

"What are your thoughts on Thelema?" Dumas asks in a gravel voice.

I shrug. "I don't really have any. I'm not a Thelemite or a Crowley-ite."

Abraham's eyes seem sharp, a slight friendly smirk spreads across his face as he watches me.

"I don't like Crowley at all," Judah shakes his head, "The man was an evil, self-centered junkie. He was a black brother. A black magician. And a pervert."

"Yes, I don't like Crowley either," Amore agrees with her boyfriend.

"Me either," Lux shakes his head.

"Crowley gave away secrets he shouldn't have," Dumas states in a blunt tone.

"I guess I don't really have anything against him. Just felt the Golden Dawn was more for me than the Ordo Templi Orientis. Or any other order I came across. I'm a nostalgic traditionalist." I shrug again, feeling like one of the Knights of the Round Table, looking around at everyone eating and discussing magick.

"Myself," Abraham chimes in, "I don't care for Aleister Crowley. What influences have you had outside the magick school of thought, Frater Parsifal?"

"I enjoy the works of Carl Jung, Wilhelm Reich, Viktor Frankl, Irvin Yalom, Nietzsche, Jim Morrison, William S. Burroughs, Brion Gysin, Arthur Rimbaud, William Blake, I don't know. There's more. I read a lot. Too much. Usually about a book a week, when I'm on top of it. I kind of have the philosophy that I should always carry a book with me, because you never know when the opportunity to read will come. In a waiting room at the doctor's office or dentist, on break at work, in the restroom, whenever. You'd be surprised how many chances to read come up during a typical day."

Abraham gives me a warm smile and a slow nod, "It sounds like a good philosophy to me."

Dumas continues to drill me with those murderous eyes. I can almost feel them piercing into me. I don't know what it is about me he doesn't like. Judah seems to get jealous of any attention I'm getting. Lucid seems to have stars in her eyes when she looks at me. She has bright brown eyes and full lips with a tight, excited smile.

Later, at the end of the evening, my wife and a couple of our friends pick me up.

I climb in to the car and sit, feeling invigorated and dazed from the experience. I have much to digest and texts to study. I can't wait to get started.

"How was it," she asks after a quick kiss, a hug, and while holding my hand, looking in my blue eyes. "You seem drained or wired or something."

I do feel different. Odd. I can't place my finger on it. Maybe the excitement of going into a house full of complete strangers and trusting them to blindfold me and stick swords to my throat. The excitement of joining the Order. It is my first experience with a group ritual rather than solo ritual work. "Yeh, baby, I guess I do feel a bit dazed or out of it."

"You are one crazy mother fucker," the driver, Barry, grins his joker grin and shakes his head.

"Yeh," his wife, Iris, the passenger looks either concerned or genuinely interested. "Tell us about it. What happened exactly? I'm not sure I understand this stuff you're getting involved in."

I light a cigarette for myself and my wife, Hillary. "I can't really say anything about what went on. I took an oath of secrecy."

'Clocks' by *Coldplay* starts playing on the car stereo.

"Wanna smoke some herb?" Barry asks with a handsome toothy grin.

"Of course," I nod.

"I could use a couple hits," Hillary remarks.

"I don't get it," Iris says. "What is this Order about? What do you do? Why the secrecy?"

Barry passes a joint back to me as we drive around town. I answer Iris, "I don't know. Do you know Kabbalah? Astrology? Tarot cards? Alchemy? It's that kind of shit." I take a hit and pass it to my wife.

"You believe in that kind of thing?" She give me a wary look.

I shrug, "I joined."

"When I was talking with this guy the other day," Barry says and passes the joint back to me again, "God, this *Coldplay* shit is kind of cheesy. Like we're all stoned having this wonderful twenty-something reunion."

Iris hits his shoulder, "I like it. It is a wonderful reunion."

"Yeah," Hillary laughs.

Barry goes on. "The other day I was talking with this guy about how he believes in God and church and shit. As he was explaining it, I realized that it's just a place where people draw strength from and that's not such a bad thing. I used to hate Christianity and church, but if it give people strength I realized maybe it's not such a bad thing. You get my meaning?"

"I do," I agree, taking another hit.
"Well, what do you guys want to do tonight?" Iris smiles.
"Party." I take a hit.
"Yeah, let's go get some beer!" Barry hoots.
"And more pot," I grin.
"Can we eat first?" Hillary asks. She is a tiny thing. Five foot two. A little scarlet spitfire.
"Oh, yeah," Barry hoots, "I know the perfect place to eat pizza! You guys hunger for pizza? They have every kind you can imagine."
"Sounds good to me," I light a cigarette and watch the city lights and pedestrians pass by out the car window.

When we return home the next evening, Hillary and I, make love. She is a bolt of lightning. We are the original sin.
Rapture. I want all of her. As we fuck I want to be one with her. I can't live without her. In the heat of the sex, the passion, I beg, "Spit in my mouth. I want all of you."
She does.
Warm sleep in bed together. Comfort and love. Soft sanctuary. Sweat turns cold. We cuddle until sleep.
About a year before my initiation I had taken up the two-edged sword of magick. I had gone through existential crisis. As a child I was raised as both a traditional Native American and an Episcopal. I whole heartily believed both spiritual systems to be true. As I approached my teen years I began to realize that the two systems did not mesh. If I were a Christian I could not be with the Great Spirit. I became angry with God. For many reasons.
I became angry with God because I blamed God for the hardships of my childhood. I could not understand how

innocence should be harmed. For example, during war time a bomb dropping on a family's home while they eat dinner.

My brother tells a story about me when I was in Junior High School. He walked up to the gas station to get a soda and candy one afternoon. Walking home through the alley all these white papers blow by. He picks one up to discover it is bible pages caught by the wind. His only thought, "What the fuck?" He approaches our house to see me standing on the roof tearing pages from the bible one by one. My anger toward God grew to rage by my late teens.

I recall driving down the street one summer evening when I was about 19 years old. My girlfriend had just broken up with me. I screamed at God. From deep in my soul I raged at the Lord. I swore at Him and challenged him to come down and face me. "Take me on! Face me now! Come on you fucking pussy! If you're up there come the fuck down here and face me now you, fucking bastard son of a bitch cocksucking motherfucking asshole!" I was punching the roof of my car as I sped down side streets. *Nirvana* blared on the stereo. Boom. My car smashed into a Mustang at an intersection. The Mustang spun into a yard. My car lost a headlight. I didn't have car insurance. I left town that night on a bad check writing spree.

My relationship with God was constant and shifting like water. A year or so later I was caught in a blizzard. I had to walk a couple of miles through the snow, wind and dark. I became so cold I felt as though I was burning up. My legs ached from treading the heavy snow. I honestly didn't know if I would make my destination. Or maybe it was just the pain and fear. That night I made a pact with God. A covenant. An oath. A vow. A promise. It was the night I took up this spiritual sojourn. The night I accepted my Grail quest. "If only I make it home." I made it home.

My next strong experience with God was on bus ride through the Rocky Mountains. It was sunrise. I had no money in my pockets. No food. One suitcase of clothes. Almost out of cigarettes. Got nowhere to go when the bus reaches its destination. Just came off the street life. Everything's going to be alright. Golden morning rays triumphed over the mountains and through the bus window, warming my face. I knew everything would be okay.

I entered a period of recluse. Found a woman to settle down with and had a star. A high school drop out, I decided to go back to school for a while, college. I took up the hobby of reading. I had always read comic books growing up. The first books I read were many of the works of Carl Jung, Jack Kerouac, James Redfield, Daniel Quinn, Viktor Frankl, William S. Burroughs, Charles Bukowski, Irvin Yalom, Lord Byron, Mary Shelly, William Blake, Frederich Nietzsche, J.D. Salinger, Samuel Coleridge, John Milton, H.P. Lovecraft, Jim Morrison, Stephen Hawkings, Albert Einstein, and many others. My mind was hungry. I was a sponge for information. My soul ached to be filled. On and on I studied psychoanalysis, alcoholics anonymous, the Arthurian mythos, *Star Wars* books, *Dungeons and Dragons* books, classic science fiction and fantasy, Buddhism, Hinduism, Christianity, Islam, Judea, Shinto, Taoism, tribal religions, Mormons, cults, and many more. Scientific explanations for creation. I became Galabram and spontaneously invoked Pan one night, naked, wearing a bone necklace, purple lip stick, and swaying to Peter Murphy music.

I come to the existential crisis. Existential angst. I was now married with more children. There is no God. God is the creation of Man. Man created God in his image. The universe was an accident. The Big Bang unexplainable, but not the divine work of God or any other higher intelligence. There is no soul, just the physical, just a brain and nervous system. Emotions are just chemical reactions. It is a cold and meaningless universe. You did not exist before birth, and you cease to exist at death. Any meaning for anything created by the thinker, all creation an accident, pure chance. When you die you die, cease to exist completely. Death anxiety creates Gods and religions, an afterlife, and so on.

This belief system did not sit well with me. It lasted about two years. I became miserable with this universal view. There seemed no point to anything in a cold and uncaring universe. I sat sad, contemplating how science could possibly prove there is a God. I didn't want to be an atheist. But to me atheism was truth, inescapable, but then truth set me free. On my bookshelf a copy of Aleister Crowley's *Magick Without Tears*. As I opened that book to its first page, I opened to the next chapter of my quest for the Holy Grail, which led to my initiation into the Order of the Golden Dawn. I figured, what the hell? I've tried everything else. I'll try Crowley's magick shit word for word and see what happens. It'll give me a new hobby, something to do. It gave me a new life. I opened Pandora's Box, tasted the enlightening fire of Prometheus, felt the bright burning starlight of Lucifer.

Magick cured my atheism or Chaos Magick, which I define as Magick all the way. The belief system the tool. Crowley a chaos magician, although the term was unheard of in his day. Nothing is True. Everything is Permitted. Do What Thou Wilt Shall Be the Whole of the Law. Love is the Law. Love under Will. As above. So below. Will to power and nothing else. Anarchy. The state of nature.

My occult studies intensify. I devour every magickal text I can lay my hands on. An obsession.

My wife and I take trips to the Golden Dawn Temple. She hangs out with Iris while I participate in lectures, fellowship and group rituals.

I enter the house. There are large diagrams of the Tree of Life and all its parts on the wall. Seated before Frater Abraham are Frater Azazel, Frater Judah, Frater Alpha and Soror Amore Delamore.

Abraham gives me a warm smile. "Frater Parsifal, glad you made it. We just sat down, the lecture hasn't begun. Some of the others couldn't make it. It's hard to find a time that works for everyone."

I nod and sit down next to Frater Azazel, his buggy eyes examining me from beneath his long straggly hair. His face thin. Cheeks sunken.

"How are you?" He shakes my hand, his grip strong and cold.

"I'm good, it was a long drive up here."

"Oh, how long of a drive is it?"

"About five hours."

"We have a few initiates that come down from Canada, but they're thinking of founding a temple there." Judah smiles, "They drive about six hours to get here."

"Uh-huh," I nod. I don't trust him, not because I think he's up to anything, but because I think he's an idiot.

"Nice shirt," Soror Amore Delamore smiles. "Where do you get something like that?"

I glance down at my old pearly buttoned cowboy shirt. "A thrift store for $1.99."

"Wow," she smiles, blonde hair and pasty white skin contrasting light blue eyes. "That's cheap. Do you buy all your clothes like that?"

"Mostly. I mix in some new stuff, too. There's just some things you can't get used."

"Like underwear," Judah laughs.

Everyone laughs.

"Yeah," I smile at Judah, "like underwear."

"Well," metro-sexual Abraham chimes in. "It's about time to proceed with the Knowledge Lecture." I imagine he makes eye contact with me longer than the other as he speaks. "The subject for this afternoon will be the ten spheres of the Tree of Life, the Sephiroth."

I sense tension coming from Judah. He feels threatened by me. Threatened because the others like me, because I seem more intelligent than him, and because his wife talks to me more than he appears to be comfortable with.

Abraham compares the Sephiroth with Plato's perfect ideas. It makes sense. The Tree of Life is a map of the universe and the soul. As above, so below. Each individual Sephirah a world/dimension or part of the soul/consciousness. As the initiate rises in grade levels in the Golden Dawn, they explore and experience a different Sephirah with each grade. There are ten grades. Neophyte being the first.

When the lecture is over we sit around chatting before the ceremony. Frater Azazel and I elect to go outside and have a cigarette before changing into our ritual robes.

We go out the back door. It's a sunny summer afternoon. The grass and tree leaves are vibrantly green. We sit on the back porch at a round table with an umbrella and light our cigarettes.

I break the ice, "So do you guys have contact with the OTO?"

Azazel raises an eyebrow and grins, he reminds me of thin Spock from *Star Trek*, with a beard and long hair. And his ears aren't pointy. "Yes. Some of us do, but most of the Golden Dawn sees them as misguided. Abraham was with them at one time. I know Judah knows some of them. Can you keep a secret?"

I nod.

"My intuition tells me I can trust you, as does your talk of Chaos Magick. I am a member of this order. If most of the others knew they would not be happy about it. They would kick me out of the Golden Dawn. Abraham and Alpha are the only ones who know, beside you now."

"You can trust me. A schism. That's stupid. Dumas is a Mason, huh?"

Azazel takes a drag of his cigarette and nods thoughtfully.

I talk in a low voice, "Listen, I know I'm not supposed to go outside my grade work, but I've studied all the texts the Golden Dawn has given me. I didn't learn anything new. I'm eager to learn more. No. I'm eager to *experience* more of what I've studied. I'll follow my Golden Dawn work and experiment on the side. I have already been experimenting with methods of Chaos Magick and shamanism. I'd like to work with someone with more experience than I have. I've succeeded with invocations. I want an evocation. What's your grade level?"

"Adeptus Minor."

"Holy shit! I've never met anyone so advanced."

Azazel laughs, "You are enthusiastic. I'll work on a side project with you."

"Cool."

"Abraham is Adeptus Major. Judah is Philosophus, actually he's in the Portal preparing to be Adeptus Minor. Alpha, Dumas, Titania, and Amore Delamore are Philosophus. Sothis is also in the Rose Cross with Abraham and me, but I don't know his grade. I think he may be higher than both of us. I think he may be in the next inner order."

"How many inner orders are there?"

"Three total. The outer order is the Golden Dawn. The inner order is the Rose Cross. Inside that is another order."

"Above that is the Secret Chiefs."

Azazel shrugs, "Maybe."

"Huh. So what about the experiment?"

"We'll do it over the astral plane. Synchronize rituals. Midnight on Friday. I'll send you information through the astral plane and you will evoke what you receive. We will trade notes later and we'll know if you received the right information or not."

"Okay. Sounds good."

"Ready to go in?"

I flick my cigarette over a fence, "Yeah."

We stand in a circle all draped in black robes, the room dimly lit with flickering candles. Judah is robed in white sitting at a small throne in the east of the temple, wielding his long staff and wearing a gold crown. The station of the Heirophant, the High Priest. But Frater Abraham is leading the ritual, designed by him. We go through typical Golden Dawn rite. I am familiar with them all and have done them all on my own, as a solo magician. The entire ritual is about an hour and a half long. An Invocation of Anubis. Anubis is invoked passing a personal message for each of us. We clear our minds and meditate. The stillness of mind. In through the astral plane comes the jackal-headed god, Anubis.

I see him coming. He is coming. There is naught but darkness! From within this sea of darkness a small swirling mist appears and grows. The thin wisp of silver mist twists and spirals into a thick fog filling the dark room. The center of the fog parts. The silhouette of a man standing, holding a long staff appears before me. Tall with ears like the *Batman*. Light shines from behind him.

The jackal god steps out of the fog. Canine feet and a stoic jackal's head with long, sharp teeth frozen in a permanent grin. His expression silent, eyes black oil, chest and arms thick, powerfully built.

Time stretches out. I'm afraid of Anubis like I'm afraid of an unfamiliar, wild dog. The old Egyptian deity raises its staff and grants me vision. I see a city of pyramids in a vast desert with many workers constructing temples. I see a young, handsome man riding a chariot, a chalice in his hand. A woman dressed in flowing red staring forlornly out a tower window. Witches burning and being tortured, raped and maimed, screaming. The massacres of Cathars, Templars, Jews, wars in the Holy Land, massacres of Native Americans, he shows me the Irish and Scottish fighting for freedom, Pancho Villa and Abbie Hoffman, Nietzsche and Jung, Darwin, Freud, Nazi SS, Tibetan monks, Antarctica, the Mojave Desert, Atlantis, Lemuria, Thule, Agarti, Shamballah, Hyperborea.

I'm shaken to my soul. The jackal-headed god gently lowers the staff and draws a flaming sword. My hands go up in surrender. The sword arcs swiftly, cleanly cutting my head off, blood flows out like a fountain. My hands grasp at empty air above my neck. My head lays at my feet gasping like a fish out of water.

I drop to my knees. Dark blood spurts from my neck with every dying beat of my heart. My robe, drenched in the hot liquid, pastes to my body.

Anubis gives a wider toothy grin and silent upward howl. The feral god lifts up my head by its hair and looks into my shocked eyes. I see his deep black eyes. Pure black. Glossy, glassy black. An endless darkness. An abyss.

He places my head on top of my neck. The mortal wound instantly healed and the blood is gone. I stand fully resurrected.

Anubis places his index finger over pursed black lips and fades back into the fog, becoming once again a wisp and then nothing.

We sit in a circle, the rite not yet closed.

In a feminine voice Frater Abraham softly says, "If any of you would like to share your experience, you may do so now."

Judah instantly speaks up with a tone of pride. "I saw Anubis and he showed me the world. He showed me pollution and litter and oil spills. He showed me rain forests being cut down. He showed me people starving and war and people dying from AIDS. Then he crushed the world in his hands and handed it to me. I opened my hands and the world wasn't crushed anymore." There are tears in Judah's brown eyes. He looks around the room searching for our reactions.

Abraham gives a warm, knowing smile, "That's beautiful, Judah. Any one else?"

Soror Amore Delamore whispers, "He had a huge cock."

"Lydia!" Judah gives a hushed cry.

"It's alright, Judah," Abraham rests his hand on the High Priest's shoulder. "It's all symbolic. You must remember to use her magickal motto in the temple."

Judah nods, his complexion red.

Amore gives Judah an innocent smile and continues. "He grabbed me and we made love. I couldn't resist him. He was so primal, so primitive. Like the strongest of the tribe. And when I came, all I saw were the stars. Like I was floating in outer space and everything was still and silent. I felt my body stretch across the universe. I became one with everything. It felt so serene. So calm. I felt like I was home in my mother's womb again."

"That is a beautiful vision," Abraham smiles. "There is much there."

"I'd like to share my sight," Frater Alpha mumbles.

Abraham nods.

"I saw myself surrounded by witches. Out west. I was a warlock. Skyclad and dancing and fucking in the moonlight. A green man appeared in the forest. There were little elves peeking around trees and little mushroom people, too. It was nice."

Abraham appears speechless.

"How about you, Parsifal," Judah challenges.

"Um, Anubis cut my head off."

"Wow," Abraham sighs.

"Then he put it back on. I kept thinking of the song by Nick Drake, 'Black Eyed Dog'."

"Morbid," Judah replies.

My wife and I ride home. Our babysitter couldn't have the kids overnight so we drive back on the highway that night. On a narrow road we come around a long curve. In one lane is a semi-truck rumbling onward. In the other lane is another semi-truck trying to pass the first. Two monstrous, metallic juggernauts grumble toward us, the wind hissing, and nowhere to escape.

I look at my wife, the panic in her face matches the panic in my throat.

I swerve off onto the shoulder and onto the edge of the ditch. The second semi slams on its brakes almost sliding into the other semi.

It is a close call. Death so close.

My wife and I just sit there breathing.

We go over the details of the near accident several times before continuing the ride home.

Our love seems so deep.

Six months earlier I had succeeded in Knowledge and Conversation with my Holy Guardian Angel. This secret is on the tip of my tongue at my Golden Dawn meetings, but I know that Judah and some of the others won't believe it. It happened during a sex magick rite with Hillary. I felt my consciousness travel through time.

I opened the pathway between my consciousness and the collective unconscious. Every bit of data stored in the DNA of my parents up to the point of conception passed on to me. Every bit of data stored in my grandparents to the point of my parents conception stored within their DNA. And so on all the way up the family tree. Back to primitive times. Cave men and women fucking. I became them all at once. Experiencing the sex that each of them had. Back to the beginning. All the way back. I became the one-celled organism reproducing. A cell splitting. I became a sperm serpent traveling within the woman, racing to the egg. I felt it around me. Wrapping me. Holding me. I was traveling a dark red tunnel. The fool of the Tarot beginning his journey. I fell into *The Tibetan Book of the Dead*.

It was an amazing experience. A triumph for me. I used Hebrew Gematria to uncover specific details of my HGA. His name is 278. An angel of Jesod which guards the gate to the Garden of Eden with a sword of flame. Kerub. Born of the mystery of Daath. Entered by the double gates. 11:11. Entered between the pillars of the Temple of Solomon. Entered by the pyramid which is 11 times 11.

I look forward to the experiment with Frater Azazel, who refers to himself as a thelemic knight. We had to postpone or experiment for some time. "Frater" means "brother". "Soror" means "sister". I've invoked things in the astral plane and done much work there. My skills with the Tarot cards is increasing as well. Astrology I work with, but struggle with. Alchemy. Pathworking. Channeling. But evocation I have not done! Evoking an entity onto the material plane, the Sephirah Malkuth.

Friday night. The night of the planned experiment of Azazel and myself. We have houseguests.
Hillary and I hide in our bedroom.
"What am I going to do, honey? This is a pretty big deal to me. I love our friends, but I have to do this ritual."
She is putting make-up on in front of the mirror. "What time are you supposed to do it?"
"Midnight."
"That's fine. Everyone will be going to bed by then. You can come in here and do the ritual in the bathroom."
We have a big bathroom in our bedroom and a second smaller bathroom the guests will be using.
"That's a good idea. The mirrors will be a definite advantage." There are four mirrors in the bathroom. Two in the north, one south, and one west.
We sit with our guests watching Japanese horror movies all night. The lights are off. In one of the films there is a gray dead girl. She sneaks around and kills people making creepy, god-awful noises. She haunts her victims before killing them. Her black hair morphs and the girl never talks. She moves at odd angles, in unnatural ways, joints clicking. A very eerie movie.
"God, this movie's going to give me nightmares," Hillary groans.
I look at the clock. "I need to go to bed." It's a quarter to midnight.

"I'm going to watch the rest of the movie." She gives me a kiss and I retire to our room.

In the bathroom I light a black incense stick and five red candles. Before me a black double cubed altar with a cup, pentacle, dagger and wand upon it. I strip naked and stand before the altar. My right hand raises high above my head, pointing the index finger skyward. "Atah…" I vibrate and drop the index finger to my forehead. "Malkuth…" Index finger at my groin, pointing down. "Vigaburah…" Index finger at my right shoulder. "Vigadulah…" Index finger at my left shoulder. "Leolahm, Amen." Hands folded at my chest.

Before me in the ether I sense a pale blue, almost white, light in the form of the cross, its two crossed lines endless.

I use my right index finger and trace a pentagram in front of me. Facing the east, "Yod Heh Vau Heh…"; facing south, "Adonai…"; facing west, "Eh Heh Yeh…"; and facing north, "Aglah." Again I face the east with arms outstretched and in a low, quiet chant: "Before me, Raphael." An archangel dimly appears in the astral plane. "Behind me, Gabriel; at my right, Michael; at my left, Auriel. For about me flames the pentagram and within me shines the star of Solomon."

I continue on with the Middle Pillar Ritual, Hexagram Ritual, and the Rose Cross Ritual. At this point I take up the Dragon Asana posture before the altar and slow burning incense. The goal is to still my mind, after having done the banishing rituals to keep out everything but Azazel's incoming data. Once the mind is still it will be much easier to receive Azazel's information.

My eyes are wide open, staring blankly, unblinking ahead through the incense smoke and into themselves in the mirror. The orange candle light flickers. After many minutes and a painful breakthrough, the itching stops, the pain of absolute stillness strived for passes away as an alternate state of consciousness unfolds. In the mirror my face blurs from wolfman into Jesus and into a clay face. The dim candle light seems so intense and bright, golden lights of an ancient, mystical city.

I'm open. I'm empty.

Come in, come in, come in.

And it comes.

In the mirror before me. It appears behind me. Its long, amphibious, skinny fingers rest on my naked shoulders. Its elongated neck as long as my head. An odd, egg-shaped head. Stoic big, black, oval eyes. Tiny slits for a mouth, nostrils and ears.

It appears in the mirror before me. I watch my own reflection's metamorphosis into the egg head alien. A grey alien. Fifteen feet tall.

The entity simultaneously stands outside our house, intangibly dipping its head through the ceiling, inspecting the bathroom.

The incense smoke swirls and takes on an egg shape. Empty holes in the smoke become its hollow eyes.

It seems to be everywhere at once. To fill everything at once.

In my head.

Somewhere. All at once.

Holding me in the palm of its hand. I'm tiny and cupped in the thing's soft hand, scientifically inspecting me like an tiny, unusual insect.

It stands before me in our yard. I'm nude, standing on the lawn with a gaunt, skyclad alien before me, reaching its slender arms toward me. Long skinny, elongated fingers. A tiny expressionless, unmoving mouth slightly open.

I don't understand what it wants. What does it want? I don't want to touch it. I don't want to touch it! It's going to embrace me. Oh, God. How did I get in my yard. The neighbors are going to call the police. Or at least think I'm a weirdo.

Wait. I'm not in my yard. I see a red triangle in the mirror. I'm in my bathroom. Never left this room.

The alien is fading away. My hands are trembling. I quickly work through a banishing ritual and blow out the candles.

I sit with my head on my knees, collecting myself, trembling.

What the fuck was that? It scared the shit out of me. Completely unexpected. Azazel could have sent a succubus or something.

The next day I sit alone, contemplating the previous night's experiment. I'm on the porch smoking a cigarette. A copy of Peter J. Carroll's *PsyberMagick: Advanced Ideas in Chaos Magick* in my lap.

I pull my cell phone out of my pocket and dial.

Ring. Ring. Ring.

"Hello."

"What the hell did you send me last night?"

"What did you get?" Azazel chuckles.

"Something frightening," I mumble.

Azazel says in a calm voice, "I sent you a triangle and a succubus."

I shake my head. "That's not what I got. I mean, I got the red triangle and thought of a succubus for the briefest moment, but what about the alien?"

"I guess we have to call it a failure then. Except for the triangle. I didn't send the image of an alien. Did you do the banishments and a complete magickal circle?"

"Shit. Of course! The alien thing wasn't just an image. It had consciousness. It was alive. I could clearly sense that."

The afternoon sun is bright and hot. I take my shirt off. I'm sweating and tan this summer. Wearing a pair of red sunglasses. Neighbor kids play in their yard across the street.

"So you saw an alien."

"Yeah. It was kind of freaky. To say the least."

"I'm sure it was unsettling. You must have opened yourself too much. It could have been some astral junk. Just a stray demon or something along that line."

"I did ample banishment."

"Something slipped in. Probably some mindless astral zombie."

"It was too powerful. It had too much of a presence. It was too intelligent to be mindless astral junk."

"An elemental, maybe."

"Maybe."

"So what are your plans now, Parsifal?"

"I'm ready for the Zelator initiation. I've been ready."

"Good. I'll tell the others. Next time we get together you'll be initiated."

"Okay."

"Studies are going well?"

"I don't care for geomancy. I'm very much enjoying working with the elements. Working on my birth chart and my genealogy. The Tarot, the LBRP, and Middle Pillar Ritual daily as a bare minimum. Magickal diary every day."

"You do seem precocious and driven."

"Thank you."

"What else are you working on? Something epic I'm sure."

"Hmm," I laugh. "You heard of Jack Parsons."

"Oh, no, Parsifal. Tell me you're not serious."

"I'm going to emulate the Babalon Working he did with L. Ron Hubbard. It will be similar in spirit to Frater TOPAN's work, but the goals and method differ significantly."

"I don't understand. To what end?"

"I call it the Babalon Isis Working. It will take seven months to complete. The primary goals are a summoning and covenant with the goddess Babalon and a series of initiations in alignment with my grade initiations. The final outcome, illumination."

"Babalon is a dangerous goddess to work with. Even with your brash enthusiasm I'm sure it's not a good idea. Hold off on this until you are in the Order of the Rose Cross."

"No. I'll be fine. I have to do it. I can feel it."

Jack Whiteside Parsons was a rocket scientist, an inventor of rocket fuel and a founding member of Jet Propulsion Labs (JPL; co-workers would some times joke that the initials stood for Jack Parsons Labs) which is a part of NASA. There is a crater on the moon named after him. He was a spiritual son of Aleister Crowley. A member of the Ordo Templi Orientis Agape Lodge in Pasadena, California. He became Master of the Temple and died under mysterious circumstances. A chemical explosion in his garage, his homemade lab. The explosion occurred as he was packing to leave for Mexico with his lover, Marjorie Cameron, where he was to develop a missile program for Jerusalem.

Jack was said to have remained eerily calm while talking to the ambulance people while they attempted to save him. He was severely burned, his arm completely blown off. His last words were said to be something like, "I wasn't done yet."

He had become obsessed with the goddess Babalon after completing the Babalon Working with the aid of L. Ron Hubbard. Marjorie Cameron was the elemental who answered the call to make a moonchild. Babalon predicted that Jack would die engulfed in flames. Some say his death was an accident. Some say murder. Some say Babalon. If a murder, different esoteric occult circles and governmental intelligence circles had motive. Funny how the esoteric circles and intelligence circles often cross paths throughout history, all the way back to John Dee, the original 007, who may or may not have been a previous incarnation of Jack Parsons.

"Sometimes I wonder if Chaos Magick is a blessing or a curse. It leaves the door open for those who may not be ready."

"I'm not ready?" I ask Azazel.

"That's not for me to say. There are some magicians that need to go slow. Most should. You are on the fast track."

"I can do this. I can handle it."

"I've seen some good magicians, good people, with lots of potential rise fast and burn out faster because they were so good at magick."

I laugh. "So now you're saying I'm good at magick?"

"You have much potential, young padawan."

"Like a schizo with a steering wheel."

"Be careful, Parsifal. Sometimes you get what you ask for."

"I will."

Part Two

The Babalon Isis Working

"I want to be a poet and I am working to make myself a seer, you will not understand this and I don't know how to explain it to you. It is a question of reaching the unknown by the derangement of all the senses. The sufferings are enormous, but one has to be strong, one has to be born a poet, and I know, I am a poet." — Arthur Rimbaud

"Let this stumbling be under your hand." — Isaiah 3:6

January

I wait until January to begin the working. It's a mild winter. Beginning the Babalon Isis Working 59 years to the hour of the original Babalon Working. The working consists of daily ritual magick. No break in the daily flow for the entire seven months. In the beginning Hermes Thoth is the focus of invocations, being god of magick and writing it seems appropriate. I begin regular invocations of my Holy Guardian Angel as well.

During an invocation of Hermes Thoth, he appears in the astral plane before me as a man with a body like the statue of David. The Caduceus staff in his hand. Winged ankles. A winged helmet. Mercury. Bright, shining blue eyes. Very handsome. I sit robed before him within my magick circle.

From the astral he reaches forward through the magick circle and takes my hand. My physical hand tingles. I'm shocked at his crossing the circle.

Holding my hand, he says, "Frater Parsifal, in the long night you will die severely. You will be dead before the dawn. The death will be poetic and your corpse draped in scarlet. The sunrise will break all illusions."

That night I dream of little grey aliens inspecting me. A typical abduction dream. Medical experiments. The Captain of the space ship is a blonde-haired German in a Nazi uniform. He stands speaking with a dirty, black-bearded Frenchmen dressed in worn chainmail and a dusty white tunic decorated with a large red cross. The German is speaking in French with the knight.

A short, grey alien approaches the two conversing figures. The slender, childlike alien seems to glide more than walk. The alien stands, looking up at the Nazi captain, their eyes locked. They stare at each other for a moment. A telepathic exchange occurring. The Nazi nods and salutes, "Heil Hitler."

The alien silently salutes back.

Now sitting on a metal bench with a black-haired man watching this exchange. My senses are fuzzy. Sequences of events are difficult to determine. But this black-haired man and I just observe the exchange between the alien, the Nazi, and the Frenchman.

"It's all about eugenics," the man whispers to me. His black hair is slicked back. "Technology. Nanotechnology. Genetics. DNA. Bloodlines. Racial purity. Making effective slaves or master races, depending on who's in charge."

"Where are we?"

"Not far from home. The dark side of the moon. If I have my bearings right."

"How could you know that?"

"I'm astral traveling. I'm not actually here. This isn't my physical body. It's made of astral substance and re-enforced with an invisible merkabah chariot."

"Who are you?"

"Frater Sothis."

"What are the chances of us running into each other here in my dream?"

"This is not a dream."

"I think it is."

"Trust me. Aliens are my specialty. I've been studying them for years. I was a part of one of the army's remote sensing projects."

"I prefer to think I'm dreaming."

"Whatever floats your boat. I thought you wanted truth."

"What are the chances of us meeting up like this?"

"You already said that. I keep an eye on all the alien activity, and you are a member of my Order. We are brothers. We must take care of each other."

"This is so strange. The aliens scare the shit out of me. They're so god damned creepy. I can't sense what they're about."

"Tell me about it." Sothis lights up a Pall Mall cigarette. "These aliens and Nazis got a thing for you, son. I don't know why. I think you brought in on yourself, with your occult experiments."

"You're Italian."

"Yes, my father was mafia. I was army and worked in underground military bases in New Mexico and Nevada. I wanted to get away from the family business and saw the military as a reliable alternative. I ended up going from one secret world to another. We can not escape destiny."

"What? That's crazy. I mean, I knew about the mafia. But aliens? Underground bases?"

He shrugs.

I raise an eyebrow. "How can you smoke in the astral plane?"

"It's a vice. I'm a chain smoker."

I shake my head, "Why do the aliens and Nazis have it out for me?"

"I was listening to them talk."

"You speak French?"

He nods. "German, Italian, Latin and Hebrew." I realize he looks like a member of the mafia dressed in a black pinstriped suit. "I'm not sure what the deal is. I couldn't hear it all, and if I get too close to the Greys they'll notice me. But apparently the Templar Knight is you in a past life."

"What?" I sit up straighten my shoulders.

"They were talking about the Templar's secret religion. An esoteric Christianity. Your bloodline and your different incarnations through the ages. An impressive list. You were Jim Morrison in your last life. Rasputin's mom in one life. Alexander the Great's mom. Nicholas Flamel. Just to name a few. You have always been someone who attempts to push humanity forward."

"Enough! This is preposterous. Absolutely ridiculous. How could my soul exist in two places at once? I don't even know if I believe in past lives."

"The soul always exists, everywhere at once. Time is nonlinear. The soul is infinite. Stretched out between all time and dimensions, all universes. It is god and your Holy Guardian Angel. You'll learn this again. Remember it. Half the problem with humans is the death anxiety caused by not remembering their past lives."

I give him a blank stare.

He continues. "The soul is immortal. A complete being containing the seed of godhood. An infinite being with infinite consciousness. The soul is in all its incarnations at once. Not just in this universe, but all of them. When you were that knight, Geoffrey de St. Omer, initiated into the Templar Knights, you attained Knowledge and Conversation with your Holy Guardian Angel and became aware of all past incarnations. You did this in other lives, too. To greater and lesser degrees."

"From your reputation I gathered you are a bit of a fruit."

"Yes," he smiles. "Others in the Golden Dawn don't believe in aliens."

"I don't know what to believe."

"Believe nothing," Sothis says in all seriousness.

The Nazi and the Templar wander off down a metallic corridor together.

"Why would I be with a Nazi?"

Sothis answers, "I am here to watch you. None of the others know I'm here. They don't know what we're about either. Not all Nazis were evil. Just like Americans. Not all Americans are evil." He gives a wide grin. "History is written by the victors. Don't get me wrong. I'm not saying the Nazis were a good thing. Very far from it. I'm saying America is just as bad as the Nazis."

"Not even Abraham knows you're watching me?"

"No. I am of higher order than Frater Abraham."

"Which order? Not the Rose Cross. Something deeper."

"We await your arrival in this life, Frater Parsifal. Be careful. There are those against you. The black brotherhood. Trust no one."

Beep. Beep. Beep.

My alarm clock wakes me.
Hillary rolls over and pulls the blankets over her head.

Throughout January I continue to invoke daily. The Black Madonna. Babalon. Isis. Diana.

During a pathworking I travel to Hyperborea. An ancient city of ice and giants. I see a scraggily, bearded man, a mountaineer climbing into a giant vagina. A black shadow appears behind me, like Conan the Cimmerian, holding an ax over his author, forcing his story to be told. "Between the elevens is the conception," the shadow whispers in my ear. "Turn back Parsifal, turn back, she comes for you. She has come. She always comes."

I realize the mountaineer is Aleister Crowley.

I invoke. I evoke. The candles burn. The incense burns. The circle is strong. I disrobe.

Before me the Virgin Mary transforms into the Egyptian goddess Isis. We make love between the two pillars. The gateway is open. 11:11 is open. The doorway is open and I let it flow. The doorway to the Illuminati. A gateway to another reality permanently opened. For anything to crawl through.

As I cum in the Virgin Mary I have a memory of myself as St. Omer fighting Muslims in a hot, dry desert. I glance to my left and see Jim Morrison looking through the mirror at the Virgin Mary and me as we fuck. Alexander the Great appears on a golden staircase between the pillars. His handsome face looks like Jim's twin. Alexander points up the golden staircase. "You are a warrior. You are what you choose to be."

On January 22 I discover a supreme secret of magick. The Lotus Wand Working.

At the very end of the month I am finally initiated as Zelator $1° = 10^{\square}$. Isis appears during the initiation rite and warns me to be weary of Lam, the gray alien Aleister Crowley spoke with and drew. My ordinary, everyday life, my job, it has all become mundane to me. The only thing in life that matters in the Babalon Isis Working and the Great Work.

February
In February I construct a magickal square to create servitors. The experiment fails. The constant rituals seem to invigorate me rather than tire me. Babalon calls me the Sun. Isis and Ra teach me of Ouroboros, the eternal serpent, eating its own tail, eating itself in a neverending circle, the circle of birth, life, death, and everything in between.

By letter, I am invited to another city by magicians of the Golden Dawn named Frater 22 and Soror 43. I am a member of the Golden Dawn Temple of Isis. They are of the Temple of Osiris. It is a three hour drive. Before receiving the letter I didn't know there was another temple this close to home.

I go by myself, leaving Hillary at home with our children.

Frater 22 sits at a piano, playing a very soft song. A white candle burns atop the white grand piano. He looks back at me and smiles, wearing a white tuxedo, "Call me Sebastian." He is very clean-cut and rich looking. Old money. Distinguished.

"Alright," I nod.

"Have a seat." Soror 43 smiles and waves a hand at the couch she's seated on. Their home is elegant. Antique furniture, expensive rugs, and wall hangings. Frater 22 has a very gothic look about him. His shoes remind me of pilgrim's shoes, with the large silver buckles. He is thin and tall. Large features in his face. He's what I imagine a warlock in an old faerie tale to look like. Or maybe the lead singer for the *Bauhaus*, Peter Murphy. He continues to play this beautiful song on the piano. A sad, noble song.

I sit next to Soror 43. She is blonde with a large nose and an immaculate body. Big blue eyes. A grace to her movement. Something wild hidden beneath the conservative surface. They both appear to be in their mid-fifties.

"Would you care for a drink," Soror 43 asks in an elegant tone.

"No, thank you, I'm fine," I mumble.

"Do you know why you're here," she asks.

"No," I quietly answer. "I thought the Golden Dawn sent me here for some ritual work and a Knowledge Lecture or something. I get the feeling that's not the case. How did you know I am a member?"

"That's right," Sebastian whistles and stops playing, turning to face me. "The Golden Dawn talks. They all gossip like any group. And remember, you are no longer a 'member', you are an 'initiate'. Understand? Of course you do, my boy."

"We know what you're doing with the Babalon Isis Working," Soror 43 purrs.

I flinch. "How could you know?"

"We are Rosicrucians," Sebastian smiles and folds his hands in his lap. "Soror 22 is quite competent with divination. Real Rosicrucians, mind you."

I open my mouth, but no words come out.

Confessions of a Black Magician

Soror 22 places her delicate hand on mine and enthusiastically says, "Don't worry, Parsifal, your secret is safe with us."

Sebastian clears his throat, "We would like to initiate you into another Order. Upon completion of the Babalon Isis Working you will be of the first grade of our Order, having been most likely advanced in your current Order's grade levels."

I scratch my ear. "Mind if I smoke?"

"By all means, smoke. There's an ashtray under the coffee table." Sebastian is sitting on the piano bench with his back to the piano now. His elbows rest on his knees. His folded hands slightly supporting his chin.

I light a cigarette. "Why would I want to join this other Order? I will get to the Order of the Rose Cross through the Temple of Isis."

"It's the Order you seek," Soror 43 smiles. "Not the Rosicrucians."

I raise an eyebrow. "Soror 22, I don't think I understand. I didn't know I sought another Order."

"Please, call me Melissah," she smiles.

Sebastian continues, "You will continue as an initiate of the Golden Dawn and continue your work with the Isis Temple. You will continue on your path to the Rose Cross. We speak of the Order of the Silver Star. If you accept, you will know only the other initiates of the order, those have initiated you. If you do accept and succeed, you will likely come to recognize other initiates through acute observation. And one day you would initiate your own disciples."

I whisper, "This Order exists? The real thing? I don't believe this."

Sebastian stands. "I'll leave Melissah to discuss the details with you, Frater Parsifal."

He walks graciously and confidently out of the room.

I give Melissah a blank stare, trying to look brave.

"Do you smoke hashish?" She asks in a confident, care free tone.

"I have a few times when I was younger."

She lights a silver, etched pipe, hits it, and hands it to me.

I hit it.

I cough.

She stands up and plays some music, not on the piano, but on a old vinyl record player across the room. I recognize the music as a remix of the song, 'Ceremony', by band *New Order*.

She turns and walks back toward me at a fast pace, stops short, a few feet from me, and begins to dance with the 80s techno music. A serpentine dance.

I take another hit of hash and watch her sway her hips with her arms raised high over her head. She's in a silk, white dress. Her shoulders are bare.

She climbs on to my lap, "You're my little canary and I love you for it, Parsifal." She kisses me hard and passionately on the lips. Soft. Taste. Touch. Our fingers interlock.

She presses her waist against mine. She kisses my neck. Licks my lips. Straddles my waist.

Around me the world seems more alive than before. The colors brighter, all the white of the room illuminating. The music crisper. Her scent sweet.

We make love on the sofa.

Afterward we lay entangled and naked together, smoking more hashish and tenderly talking.

"I don't usually let people see me naked unless I'm drunk." She smiles and lights a cigarette.

"Oh, why not? You're absolutely beautiful, stunning. I mean, your body is sacred."

"Thank you." She smiles and has trouble looking me in the eye.

"Will Sebastian be mad?"

She chuckles, "Neither Sebastian or I are committed to anyone romantically."

"Oh. I thought he might come in here and beat me up or something."

"Yet you lie here, regardless." She smiles.

I shrug.

"You are so cute. I'm glad we've met."

"Me, too. But you're much more beautiful than me."

"Such an naive angel, Parsifal," she giggles.

"An angel?"

"We need to go soon," ignoring my question.

"Where?"

"To the ceremony."

"What ceremony? My initiation?"

"You'll see."

"What is this Order? It's not what I thought is it? Nothing ever seems to be when I find it. All mysteries lose their flavor when solved. Besides I never agreed to join."

She takes a moment, strokes my cheek, looks deep in my eyes, crow's feet around her eyes. "It's the silver, the morning and the evening star, my lover. The sun dog. The sun of red and black and silver."

Sebastian bursts in the room jubilantly, "It's time." He seems to take no notice of our nudity. "We must robe and enter the temple."

As I change into the black robe they provided for me, I wonder if sex with Melissah is part of my initiation. Was I supposed to have sex with her? Or was I supposed to turn her down? Maybe it had nothing to do with anything. What about Hillary?

We travel in a shiny black car. Driving downtown. The street lights have turned on. The sun is gone but its last rays gasp at the night as the car parks at an old, brick Masonic Temple. Sebastian is the driver. I'm in the back seat. Melissah's in the passenger's seat.

"What is this ceremony about?" I ask, feeling nervous.

"It's a special ceremony," Sebastian smiles. "You'll see when we get inside."

"You rented a Masonic hall for this?"

"No," Melissah smiles, looking back at me.

"The Order is Masonic?"

"It is a distant relative of the Freemasons." She tilts her head as she answers me.

They both wear white robes. I'm wearing the black robe.

"Time to go," Sebastian orders, shutting the car off.

We get out and walk toward the old, distinguished building. "So you're both Masons?"

Melissah kind of shrugs and purses her lips, not looking at me.

An elderly man unlocks a front door, letting us in. This is a private party. I notice he wears a Masonic ring.

Inside the Temple there must be between 100 and 200 people. Most are seated in a large circle around the room. It's hard to explain. The room looks like a gymnasium. The people are seated on bleachers. Is this the Masonic temple we entered? The sign on the building says it is.

All the people are robed. Black robes. Red robes. White robes. Yellow robes. Grey robes. Blue robes. Everyone is hooded except for Sebastian, Melissah, and me.

A priest stands at an altar in the east, chanting. He moves his hands through a series of motions as he sings and prays. The people all rise together and walk in a clockwise circle around the room, led by the priest. We follow.

When we approach the priest, the procession stops. I stand there before the priest, unsure of what to do or what to expect. There is a gold triangle on his chest. He wears a robe of white. I glance at Sebastian and Melissah, who both seem to simply watch for my reaction to the situation.

The priest says to me in a quiet voice, "Do what thou wilt shall be the whole of the law, love is the law, love under will. Every man, woman, and child is a star."

I just look at him.

He continues, "Crowned and conquering child. Knight of swords, take up your sword and rise a knight. Wield the sword of freedom with responsibility, with true will."

Without thinking, I respond, "I will and do."

The priest nods once. "Welcome, Frater Parsifal."

Melissah takes my left hand in her right hand. Her skin is soft. Her fingers gentle. I can smell her sweet perfume.

We walk away from the people, toward the exit, where we came in.

The procession begins anew. The priest takes his robe off, standing naked with a large wood phallus strapped over his groin. I look at Melissah with my mouth hanging open, "What's going on here?"

"Our part of the ceremony is over. It's time to leave. Time for you to go home." She's leading me away with her hand.

The people have stripped their robes, but all remain masked. Naked men and women circle round and round. The priest takes up the lead of the procession and they begin a snake dance. All the people begin to chant and shout. I don't recognize the language. They dance and twirl. Some couples start fucking. It becomes a large, moving orgy.

I can't look away.

We walk out the door.

Back at their home, Sebastian goes inside without saying a word to me.

I stand on the sidewalk, in my robe, next to Melissah. "What's happening? I don't understand? What kind of initiation was that? Help me understand, Melissah, please."

"Don't worry, my Parsifal," she says in a patient voice, "You've done all you need to do tonight. It was not initiation. It was an introduction. Your initiation is the Babalon Isis Working. Go home now, Frater. You will be contacted."

"You and Sebastian are members of the Illuminati? The Great White Brotherhood?"

She gives me a sad smile and gives me a slow kiss on the cheek, whispering, "Go home, little canary."

She turns and walks into the house.

I stand on the sidewalk for several minutes before getting in to my car and beginning the long drive home.

I return home and say nothing of the experience to anyone. Talking on the phone with others of the Golden Dawn, I don't mention any of it. A few days later I invoke my guardian angel again. I reach gnosis by vibrating the magickal word 'Abrahadabra'. The angel Galabram tells me a hard war is coming, but I will survive in the end. He tells me to meditate with the Strength card of the Tarot.

I sit within my magickal circle. Before me the angel Galabram speaks in a melodic voice, "You shall work with the Scarlet Woman Babalon. My number is 11:11. Work with a scryer. I am a star god archangel. We are the Serpent, let Crowley be the Beast. The Serpent and the Beast. The Serpent and Babalon have given birth to seven who will feed off of the enemies, those who attack shall be cast down and fed to the seven who are the seven sons of Galabram and Babalon, Moon and Indigo Children, they shall protect the people and the blood lines of Galabram, the Serpent King, the Exterminating Angel, the avenging angel, follower of true will like destiny, like dynasty, protector of life and wife, of mother and father, eternally, seven loyal warriors, Knights of the Temple of Galabram who is Abra, bonded, Abraham and Galahad, in union pushing back the Black Brotherhood and all Inquisitions. All shall be revealed to those who have eyes to see. There is no need for churches, there is no need for congregations, there is no need for missionaries or converts, all who come, come of their own free will, the true will answered leads all down the correct path, Chaos Magick means that all paths are valid, nothing more, fear not the wink of life, forward, Galabram parts the way. Invoke frequently."

This communication is sealed with a six point star sigil. A picture of three triangles touching at a single point in the center.

"Maranatha."

March

Rituals continue every day. Seven days a week.

On the fourth day I perform the Birthing Ritual.

It begins with a ritual cleansing, a relaxation ritual, the Lesser Banishing Ritual of the Pentagram, the Banishing Ritual of the Hexagram, and other typical Golden Dawn rites.

A strobe light is used with the recorded repetition of a woman's orgasm screaming, "Oh, god, yes, I'm coming" as Parsifal continuously copulates with the invoked goddess Isis.

This ritual plays out the drama of the sun god Khepri Ra, Helios Atum. I enter the Womb of Babalon. Parsifal dies. Natas is secretly born.

"In this you will die, which is initiation."

The lotus dies twice and the lotus is eaten as a holy sacrament.

A state of mind I can only describe as ego-less dreaming is achieved.

Babalon incarnates into mortal form on completion of the Birthing Ritual.

A woman with curly, long, fiery red hair stands in a gallery next to a painting of William Waterhouse's *The Lady of Shallot*. Her body is voluptuous and her eyes pierce my soul. She does not know what she is.

I introduce myself, exhausted from the Birthing Ritual. "Hello."

"Hello," she says in a shy voice.

"This is one of my favorite paintings."

"I like it," she smiles. "She looks so sad."

"It's Elaine. She's about to commit suicide because she's fallen in love with Sir Lancelot, but he doesn't return her love. Just like Uther did with Arthur's mother and Morgana did with Arthur, Elaine uses magick to seduce Lancelot. They conceive a child named Galahad. He becomes the greatest of the Knights of the Round Table. The purest knight. He stays a virgin his entire life to make up for his conception out of wedlock. He is the knight who finds the Holy Grail. Lancelot is in love with Guinevere, so he doesn't love Elaine. Elaine commits suicide. I can't remember if he even knows that she loves him."

She looks sad. "That is a sad story."

"Yeah."

I fall in love with Babalon incarnate instantly. I can think of nothing but my goddess, my lover, Babalon.

Twenty-one days later.

Within a garden of the dead. Sunlight beats down like a lover in heat. Corpses planted beneath our feet. We walk through the cemetery together in the afternoon. It's nice out.

Serenely, I walk at Babalon's side. Now I'm the Beast. Now I'm complete.

Her face calm. Her hair swimming in the afternoon breeze. Birds serenade. Surrounded by marble and granite headstones and statues. A necropolis of serenity. Faeries, fauns, and squirrels play and chatter around us, just out of sight in the trees and leaves. Hundreds of mute ghosts gaze at the memory of life.

We pause before a statue of Saint Francis.

"He's my favorite saint," I whisper.

Her face turns gently to me. The peace and quiet before the immaculate storm.

Her tender voice. "Talk to me."

"Mm," I shrug and leisurely slip my hands into my pockets as we continue our stroll. "About what?"

"Anything. I like it when you talk with me. I feel comfortable with you. I feel safe with you."

"I've contacted the invisible masters."

She gives a single, subtle nod.

A rabbit freezes, caught staring as we pass a mausoleum.

I continue. "Through the ether. I lost time. Gained an hour that wasn't there. They wouldn't speak to me. They laughed at me, without actually laughing. I felt like an insect among men. It was a trip. Far out."

Babalon gives another graceful nod, and in her beautiful voice asks, "Have you read the story of Faust?"

"No. I mean I know the story. Everyone knows the story. But I haven't actually read it."

Her lips form a small, sad smile. "I saw Lucifer fall from Heaven on the second day of creation. He is the most beautiful thing I will ever see. The most beautiful angel. I love him like no other."

A single tear drops from her cheek on to a rose petal before a tombstone which reads, '1947–1974'.

She continues. "It was the first time I saw the color blue. I felt such awe in the purity of that color. It was the first color I ever saw."

"You followed him?"

"Many did. A third of the Heavens. He was our leader. I had to follow him. When he fell, he fell with my heart in his hands."

"And when you fell?"

"Saw the color red for the first time."

"Wow."

"Natas," her strong, soft hand on my cheek, "you are mortal." Her endless eyes capture me, burn through my soul. "I am a goddess."

Eight days later I see the Ark of Covenant in the astral plane.

On the ninth day of the month I become Theoricus $2° = 9^{\square}$.

Four days later, a walk outside with Babalon.

The next night a phone conversation with Babalon.

The next afternoon a conversation and drive with Galabram and the prophet Abraham.

Since seeing Babalon I have begun seeing nymphs, faeries and succubi. Astral junk as well.

Easter.

Ritual: Evocation of the Star Seed. During the ritual I see and feel white warm light above me. The white light is a spirit. Successful star seed transmission. Communication with praeterhuman intelligence, like always.

Afterwards, I go to a gas station and as the clerk hands me my changes he says, "Me and my girlfriend initiated the ritual of the bunny."

I just look at him and nod, completely baffled and spooked by his statement. It is a strange thing to say to a complete stranger. I have never seen this clerk before (or since at the time of the completion of this text). It was the only thing ever said between us. Mindboggling me.

The next day I meet with my medicine man who always says he's not a medicine man, although everyone else in his tribe says he is.

"Hello, dog soldier." I shake his hand. A small dome covered with blankets stands on the ground next to us, his inipi, sweatlodge. A fire pit burns with 24 stones in it. I'm here just to talk today. Sometimes I sweat with him.

"Hello, Peta Manipi." He gives me a big smile and shakes my hand. "You have a cigarette for me?"

"Yeah." I hand him a cigarette. I smoke *American Spirits*.

"What brings you out today?"

"Nothing much."

"You are thinking about something."

He often helps me interpret my dreams. He wants me to become a medicine man. I haven't told him about my occult adventures.

"Can you make things happen?" I ask.

"Everyone can," he smiles.

We sit on tree stumps before the fire.

"You know what I mean, like magick. Can you make things happen. I know you can talk with spirits."

"I see many things, Peta Manipi. Everyone can, they just forget as they become a part of the white man's world. You and I remember how to do it."

"So you can make things happen. I wasn't sure if there was such a thing as Indian magick or not."

"Yes, I can make things happen, but it's a dangerous thing. Not usually a good thing."

"Making things happen is evil?"

"Not always. We call it shooting medicine."

"If someone shoots medicine at you, how do you protect yourself?"

"Use protection. Prayer ties. Tobacco ties. Carry the prayer in a red cloth until the feeling passes."

"Okay."

On the last day of the month I perform the Practicus $3° = 8^\square$ Ritual. Just when I think I can't endure the ritual any longer, it ends.

I am the phoenix.

April

Everything becomes a blur. Life becomes a dream.

The Pope dies.

I miss work for the first time, to stay home and continue ritual work.

In the middle of the month I take the grade of Philosophus $4° = 7^{\square}$ and dedicate the Temple of Pan. My own secret temple hidden in a forest outside of the city.

Some time later Babalon asks if I want her.

Near the end of the month I invoke Lucifer, take the station of the Beast, and become Adeptus Minor $5° = 6^{\square}$.

I am ronin. I am chaos. I am anarchy. I no longer fear Lucifer.

May

The non stop ritual work continues.

In a dream Frater Sothis appears to me. He wears black sunglasses, a black suit and tie. I sit under a willow tree reading *The Book of the Law*.

"Hello, Parsifal," he says in a casual tone, his accent revealing the slightest New York accent.

"Hi, Sothis, how are you?"

"Fine. Thank you for asking."

"What brings you to my dreaming Jesod this time?"

"I've come to say good bye." He lights a cigarette.

"Where are you going?"

"I'm catching a plane to Area 51."

"Why?"

"I'm required to check in there at times."

"I don't want you to go."

"I won't be around to watch you anymore. I won't be returning."

"I know."

"They haven't told me that, but I know I won't return."

"What will happen to you?"

"I'm not sure. They may take me to the Hollow Earth. They may kill this body. They may brainwash me. It's hard to say."

"Are you afraid?"

"No."

"I am."

"How come?"

"How do you change the world? Infiltrate the Illuminati. How do you save the world? Infiltrate the Illuminati and destroy them. The more I discover, the more my mind changes. Maybe they shouldn't be destroyed."

"It's an old war."

"The magician is the paradox. The man god. The magician knows he can not know God. Knowing of the unknown God is the link to knowing. Becoming the man god. Illuminati."

"When the magician goes so far."

I nod.

"Take care, Parsifal. We may or may not meet again."

"Good bye, Sothis."

A night alone with Babalon and Galabram.

All dreams mean something. The further back (in) you look at chaos, the more it makes sense, more order is seen the bigger the picture gets. There is too much emphasis in culture on maintaining order. Order is a natural state. It exists whether or not we enforce it with laws, dogmas, rules and authority. Theoretically this adds to the plausibility of anarchy as a system of government.

I sit here listening to *The White Stripes*. Stoned immaculate, out here we is…

There's almost a dizziness to it. My lips are numb and cold. Makes me wonder what was in the crystals.

I can write any where, any time, any how. I can do any thing. I will any thing.

I am Illuminati now. Illuminati can carve and crush empires if they will. My books are time bombs. In posthumous condition I will attain.

I saw a movie in which *The White Stripes* discuss Nikola Tesla over coffee.

Who am I?

Where am I?

Am I in this room?

Am I in the music? The sounds?

This shit really knocked me on my ass. Cold sweats, dizzy, light headed, shortened attention span, lethargic, tired, fighting passing out.

Nowhere, nothing.

Now is the time.

While in the void.

Move/expand consciousness.

I ate hair in a ritual today.

I trick myself into thinking my consciousness only expands to the line of my vision, but when I close my eyes, consciousness is still there, not changed at all, other than lack of visual input.

Cross time.

Wet vagina, two fingered clit rubbing invocation of the beast.

Long range.

Babalon bites down hard, clenching her teeth as she cums. It's dark in the motel room. She rubs her clit until she cums, enjoying and imagining 666 riding her.

She lays in silence catching her breath, staring at the speckled ceiling. What was she doing? What was she doing, has she gone crazy? Babalon succumbs to no man.

In the akashic I smile. "I am no man."

What is killing you? Guilt? Irresponsibility? Laziness? Change it. Quit worrying. Might as well try to fart your way to the moon. Act. Move. The most powerful strokes are single. One star in sight.

Galabram becomes visible in the astral plane next to me.

The Book of the Law is short. This was smart. Attention spans have shortened.

Outside this night there is lightning, an electric storm, cool, humid, gray and cloudy.

Hillary sleeps soundly.

Babalon's voice echoes. "Can you turn that down?"

I turn *The White Stripes* off and listen to the rain.

I see astral junk. Black critters, quick, low, tracers, rodents, scamper around the living room.

The Book of the Law is a call to Illuminati.

Babalon says, "There is a tornado coming."

I've become used to her appearing out of nowhere, reading my thoughts, talking in my mind, physically showing up at coincidental moments.

I am a false prophet.

I am Horus, the sun god, the child god.

I grow to become the elder sun god of resurrection.

I die to become lord of the underworld and rise again as the morning star, Lucifer, rising after the Fall.

I am two…the sun and the moon…split to unite as one…as the moon Babalon is…Isis…

I am the prophet of Lucifer-Horus and Babalon-Isis.

The more you learn, the greater the perspective, the more chaos makes sense, the more meaning is revealed.

Another day.

I sit in my car in Wal-mart's parking lot. The engine is running. There is a heavy rain coming down. The window is cracked to let the cigarette smoke roll out. Rain water sprinkles in on my face and arm. The car and street lights sparkle and blur through the watery windows.

I pick up my cell phone again.

I set it back down.

With a prolonged sigh I pick it up again and hit the call button.

The phone rings once. Twice. Thrice.

"Hello?"

"Frater Abraham?"

"Yes."

"It's me, Parsifal. Frater Judah told me to call you after reading a letter I wrote to the Golden Dawn. They said you've been assigned to help me."

"Oh, Parsifal, yes. I'm so glad you called. I volunteered to be the one who helps you. I've had experience with this sort of thing before. In fact, I used to be with the Ordo Templi Orientis."

"Really? I didn't know that."

"Yes. I've lost many friends to that path. You see, what most people forget about Aleister Crowley's system of magick is that only the strong survive. It's a fine system as long as you are one of the strong. The problem is that you don't know if you are one of the strong until it's too late."

"I see. Frater Abraham, I'm glad you are the one assigned to help me. I don't know what to do. I'm afraid. I've been contacted by the Order of the Silver Star. In order to become one of them I have to follow through with the Babalon Isis Working. I don't know what to do. I think it might be too late. I guess I just wanted to know if magick was real. I became an atheist and was so miserable living in a cold, accidental universe. I thought if I summoned the Devil and he showed up, it would prove there is a God. It would prove there is more to this life than nothingness. To make a long story short."

"All the members of the lodge became worried about you when you started to talk about aliens."

"Magick works, Abraham."

"I know it does, but there is a more peaceful way than Thelema or Chaos Magick. Why don't you tell me what happened."

"Basically I started this working to summon Babalon into my life and she showed up. Now I don't know what to do. The Silver Star seem to like what I'm doing."

"They are an extreme order of sex magicians. Weirdos. I suggest you stay away from them. Far away from them. I can't express to you how weird they are."

"Well, the fuckers give you a project, an assignment, with no instructions. You make the right choices with the project, you're successful, and you're in. If not, you never hear from them again. Now I don't know whether I should continue with the Babalon Isis Working or not. To continue means to cross the Abyss. To give up my life and everything in it to become something else. Now Babalon is here to lead me across the Abyss, but I love my wife and children. I don't want to lose them, but if I do it and succeed, can't I have it all? Whatever I want? Can't I get them back? If I am Illuminati?"

"Illuminati?"

"Ubermensch."

"Slow down, Parsifal," Frater Abraham hushes me. "Ask yourself, what is Babalon?"

"The Sacred Whore, Binah."

"Exactly. She is nothing more than a whore. Why do you want to be with a whore?"

"Okay," I mumble.

"Now listen to me, Parsifal," he says in a calm, controlled tone. "The Order wants you to turn over your magickal journals for review. We want you to write an essay explaining your reasons for wanting to stay a member of the Order, and we want you to continue your grade work. Your grade work and nothing more. Understand?"

"Okay. I'll do it."

"Good. Call me tomorrow around the same time and we'll talk and see how you're doing. I want you to promise you'll call me tomorrow and mail your journals tonight."

"Okay. I promise."

"Tomorrow we'll talk about healing you. For now just do LBRPs. Nothing else, until we can figure this whole messy thing out."

"Thank you. I knew when I met you I felt a connection to you."

"I know. Don't worry. Everything is going to be fine."

"Okay. Thanks. Good bye."

"Good bye."

After hanging up the phone, I sigh and light another cigarette. Through the pattering rain I hear the seductive voice of Babalon whisper, "Don't give them your journals. They're jealous of your genius."

I can have it all. I can do this.

The next evening, instead of calling Frater Abraham back or mailing my journals or writing an essay, I mail my resignation to the Order of the Golden Dawn.

Dear Brothers and Sisters,

I have chosen Babalon and the Silver Star. I hope we can still be friends and fellow magicians. Please accept my resignation with no ill will.

Fraternally,
Parsifal

They accept my resignation and cease all contact with me. They do not answer my phone calls or letters anymore.

I sit in a staff meeting at work. I'm anxious for it to be over, like usual. Seems like such a waste of time. Suddenly the feeling of déjà vu over takes me as I watch and listen to my boss talk. I can't focus on what he's saying. Unknown to me, this is the last staff meeting I will ever attend.

Galabram: "Levitikon!" ("Lineage!")

June
    The Devil plays my heart like a harp.
    I miss several days of work, to work with my magick.
    Hillary and I have begun to have frequent arguments about nothing important.

I sit with a friend visiting from England, having coffee, smoking cigarettes. The sun is setting. My cell phone rings. I look at it. Babalon. It's 11:11 pm. "I have to take this."
    My friend nods.
    I answer and walk down the street. "Hello?"
    "Parsifal?"
    "Yes."
    "I have to see you."
    I glance at the address of the house I'm standing in front of. 1111.

Confessions of a Black Magician

"Please, Parsifal. I'm freaking out. I love you. I need you."

"Not tonight. I'll meet you at the Temple of Pan tomorrow."

"Thank you."

The next day I sit in my desk at work. My cell phone rings again. This time it's a text. "Meet me outside."

I don't recognize the phone number.

I walk outside. It's uncomfortably hot outside.

I look around the parking lot. A man with a black moustache and tight curly hair sits in a black car. The window rolls down. "Get in."

I do.

"Do I know you?" I ask, feeling a bit afraid.

"No," he shakes his head. His hands grip the steering wheel. The car engine is running. I notice he is wearing a silver ring with the emblem of the Masons on it.

"You're a Mason." I gesture to the ring.

"Thirty-second degree. My father was thirty-third degree."

"What do you want with me?"

"Babalon is my daughter. I don't understand what you're doing to her."

"I'm not doing anything to her."

"She was normal six months ago."

"What do you mean?"

"She's changed. She was normal before. Getting straight A's in college. She's a freshman, you know. Six months ago she started acting odd. Sometimes I look at her and it's my daughter, but it's not my daughter. Her name isn't Babalon but she refuses to answer to any other name."

"What's her name?"

"Kay."

"It's a nice name. I don't understand what this has to do with me?"

"I know she trusts you. I know she meets with you. I know she talks with you on the phone a lot. Contact with you is when she changed."

"What do you want me to do?"

"Stay away from her."

"Okay. I'll stay away."

"Get out of my car."

I get out and watch him drive away.

Late in the afternoon I drive out to the Temple of Pan. As I pull up I see Babalon sitting on a large gray stone. Her waist-long hair and ankle-long skirt blow in the summer breeze. She squints to see me. She has perfect posture. As I walk to her, I realize she is the twin of the woman in the painting, *The Lady of Shallot.*

"Hi," I greet her with a smile. "I met your father today."

"What did he want?" She rolls her eyes.

"For me to stay away from you."

"He's a fucking asshole. I hate him. Don't listen to anything he says." She sits perfectly still, except for the blowing hair and skirt. She wears a blue bikini top. Her skin smooth and tan as honey, her complexion divine.

"Yeah, he seemed like a jerk."

"What's happening to me, Natas?" Her eyes plead.

"I don't know what you mean."

"Do you want me?" She licks her lips and stands close to me.

I look at the ground. Her sandaled feet. Her bare, slender toes.

"Do you want me, Natas?"

I nod, keeping my shy eyes on her little toes. I can smell her. I look up at her face. Beads of sweat sparkle across her forehead.

She speaks with a quiet voice. "I'm afraid if I kiss you again, you won't like me anymore."

"No, that will never happen."

She gently touches her lips to mine.

The kiss is everything. Butterflies in my stomach. Ice cream melting in the sun. A dream.

She whispers, "I've been thinking about you a lot."

I whisper back, "I've been thinking about you, too."

My hands rest on her hips.

She stands on her tiptoes and presses her cheek to mine, "Promise me some day I'll wake up in bed next to you."

"I promise."

It is like nothing I've experienced before. We invoke Pan for nine hours. We make love on the rock. We run barefoot, skyclad through the trees. We make love on the grass and in the dirt. Naked, we wade through the stream. We laugh and pant and gasp and roar and call out to the heavens and the sky and sun.

During her final orgasm, as the sun sets, she sings out in ecstasy, "Evoe! Evoe! IO! IO! To Pan, to Pan, to Pan! Pan! Pan! Evoe! IO! IO! To Pan!"

Riding me, she collapses forward on to my sweating, heart-beating chest, and we sleep into the summer night.

And what is life, but something beautiful when I look at you.

The next afternoon, I drive around whistling.

The cell phone rings.

I answer. "My baby, Babalon."

"Hi," she says in an unsure, hesitant voice.

"What's wrong?"

"I can't be with you Natas."

"What are you talking about?"

"It won't work."

"What are you talking about? I've made the choice to cross the Abyss for you! To cross Styx for you! Everything for you. Every love song to you. All of my love to you."

"I'm sorry."

"You're leaving me, Babalon?"

"Yes."

I start to cry. "I love you."

"I know." Her voice becomes robotic.

"Don't you love me?"

"No."

"You said you love me."

"I don't love you. Don't call me."

I am speechless.

She continues, "Good bye, Natas."

She hangs up.

Babalon succumbs to no man.

I begin fasting.

"No," Hillary lies in our driveway alone, screaming and crying. "No! No! Why did you do it? I loved you, Natas! No. No! No!"

She cries and cries and wails until her head aches and her face is red and puffy.

My life has suddenly been rocketed into a chaotic tailspin heading down to crash. The only thing I see is the ground rushing toward me. I can do nothing but sob. I'm in shock. I can't believe any of these things are happening. I think it can't get any worse. I brainstorm all available options. I could sell my car and escape to India with a friend who is about to go there himself and leave all this behind. Another option is suicide. A third option is to sell my car and buy all the drugs I can find, do them all, and just see where I end up when it's over. In a matter of days I lost more than I ever thought I had. I drive around for hours getting high and stuck, feeling overwhelmed and suffocating in a thick, black blob of hopelessness. My wife calls and asks me to come home to talk with her. I do it. When I get home I cry. She tells me she loves me and everything will be okay. I believe her.

I'm locked up in the hospital for five days.

When I get out I quit my job. I sneak in and clean my office out in the middle of the night and leave a note for my boss.

Hillary and I argue. I throw my wedding ring on the ground and it shatters.

I perform a simple ritual and take up the asana god posture. The mantram repeated in my mind is YHVH.

It's hard not to think.

Not moving comes easier.

Not sure what's happening.

White outs.

Visions come.

Mundane visions of people at work.

My consciousness seems to disappear.

A female, not quiet human, appears in mid-air before me. Pale greenish skin. A vagina on her forehead. She suddenly lunges forward and licks my forehead.

The family dog starts barking frantically when she plunges at me and breaks me from the asana.

Something very real just happened.

I'm scared. Covered in goose bumps.

A letter arrives in the mail. It's from Melissah. She tells me she dreamt I was the Pope. There is no return address. I drive back to the house where I met her and Sebastian. No curtains in the windows. It's empty. A "For Sale" sign in the front yard.

In Jesod I visit a house Aleister Crowley lived in. I discover instructions for a secret ritual he did there. It's hidden behind a still-life oil painting of fruit. There are three black rectangular disks standing behind the painting.
"Ahem," a creaky voice.
I turn and face the Master Therion, Aleister Crowley, himself.
I just look at him.
He just looks at me.
He points me to a Ouji board sitting on a small table.
I walk to it and place my hands on it. He sits on the floor across from me, our knees touching, the board resting on our knees. We scry together.
The board spells out: "Do not trust Illuminati, not trust anyone, they will hit you where it hurts."

I love the smell of my own stink. I love her stink, too. I love her. I know she loves me, too. This is quite a quiet adventure. Babalon invades everything. A haunting, red, hot angry glare. She is in my love. She is in Hillary now.

I lost everything. That woman. She has said that she is in love with me many times. I fucked her many times. I'm a little worried about cumming in her. Oh well. She said she likes my cock. Anyhow, I had to split. Broke her heart. I'm sure she'd take me back, if I'd ever want to. If ever. Remember what you did to me? That knife threat? You should never do that to someone more powerful than yourself. The woman I've been talking about is Babalon.

Things begin to turn off and on by themselves at home. Lights. Televisions. It frightens Hillary. She asks me to give up drugs and magick. I refuse.

July
I eat the flesh of God. The "final act" of the Babalon-Isis working.
God damned god tastes like shit. Where is God?
It's true. I am God.
Why does nothing make sense?
The scientists and philosophers and religions have been trying to figure shit out for years. The reason they can't is because there is an intelligence veiling everything. Preventing them from figuring it out. We are in a box. Reality is the movie. *The Matrix*. It's not robots though, it's a higher intelligence.
Why am I afraid?
The Gnostics knew, and the mystery schools!
But what did they know?
What am I looking for?
Love. I was unloved as a child. I always strive for it but there is nothing I can do. Never will be able to. As above, so below, life is a playground. My playmates and I will rule.
What is that thing you've always been searching for? A mother's love? A father's?
Ah, that's why I was a slut.

Don't trust anyone with Babalon. She hasn't gone away like she said she would.
The world belongs to the silent.

I sit alone. Feeling angry and lifeless. Deep within the Abyss. All I see is darkness and black.

I'm cold and sweating. Sleepless. My jaw aches. I don't want to be here anymore. I don't want to do this anymore. I'm sorry. I want this to stop.

It's far too late.

Unholy screeching begins. Ear piercing, hair raising, unnatural, inhuman wailing coming from all around. Soul crushing.

Covering my ears, the horrid sound is not even muffled. Choronzon is come.

I am filled with utter horror and terror as I stare back at myself.

He, Choronzon, is pure ugliness, pure hate and anger, pure ego, pure selfishness.

The battle enormous.

I hate myself.

I spent miserable time trying to stop the wheels of motion. Trying to prevent the loss of all. Trying to erase my work in Jesod, the astral, the akashic.

I should have read Faust.

I fail entirely.

Babalon is angry with me.

All Scarlet Women are avatars of Babalon while assuming this station.

Work with the Scarlet Woman Babalon is using the sexual drives as a magickal and creative force.

The intent of the original Babalon Working was to produce the daughter of Babalon, a moonchild. It opened the way.

Babalon is scarlet fire.

The crimson rose of 49 petals is a symbol of Babalon.

Technically speaking, when the magician attains gnosis and other altered states, he/she is no longer experiencing ordinary human cognition, but instead superhuman or even godlike cognition.

Babalon has walked away from me, into her own woe and internal inferno. She is prisoner of herself.

And now I feel numb, as if standing before the end of the world.

I am dour and depressed.

I have not slept in days.

It may be that Babalon is Sophia and I do love Babalon, my goddess, my beloved.

Babalon, my love, the scarlet woman, the sacred whore, the avatar of the eleventh hour.

Babalon riding the Beast is union and gnosis of true will.

Babalon, great mother, mother of abominations.

In working with a scarlet woman, she should always maintain her freedom and true will. Her body should not be given because most who now do this work are unworthy of her. Let only the scarlet woman choose her partner.

Babalon gathers pure spirits and weaves them into her flame. Their souls are seen in her ruby eyes, mighty sorceress, lust of the spirit.

Nuit is mother of Babalon.

Eat the feast prepared by the will of Babalon and see God.

Babalon, the lady of the night.

Pour my blood in the grail of Babalon to be born of her sacred womb.

All glory to Babalon, Binah.

I am no longer of this Earth.

The mystery of Babalon, mystery of mysteries, the beauty of Babalon.
Babalon is the womb of all life.
Her number is 7 and 49 and 156.
The Beast give all power to Babalon.
Babalon, draped in scarlet and violet, gold, gems, and pearls.
Babalon, bride of chaos, her holy womb and vagina the secret chalice of the Christ. The anointed one.

Sleep deprivation tends to cause hallucinations which I tend to think of as (the waving trees, melting, expanding, retracting houses) glimpses beyond the illusion of reality and astral junk.
On this day I sense the presence of Babalon and feel as though she is happy with these transactions.
NOX. The Night of Pan is a stage of ego death.
Galabram is the gnostic daemon, the poetic genius.
Babalon is love, her love is one and infinite.
Babalon is the mystery of sex and death.
Babalon, my animus.
Galabram is 278.
Sleep deprivation continues, I will sleep tonight and return to ordinary consciousness. My hands tremble as I write this.
Yesterday, experiencing such revelations and intimacy with Babalon and Galabram, was...I am unable to find the words to express the experience. I was not alone in the universe, not macrocosmically or microcosmically. Now that the communion has faded, I feel an emptiness being unable to connect and communicate so intimately, both goddess and angel continue to exist, I am simply blind and finite again.

The finite of the physical and human consciousness is sorrow. Sorrow is the vision of Binah, Babalon.

In this hollowness, felt from lack of conscious awareness of Babalon and Galabram, I realize I was abandoned today so I can find my own way. Babalon is not portrayed in true character within the occult underground. She is not the whore in the modern sense of the word. She is mother and lover of all because this is her role of creation in Binah. She is sex and she is death. She must destroy as she creates to continue the eternal flow of existence.

If the destruction of Babalon were to stop, existence would cease to exist. Babalon also remembers before time, when there was nothing and this memory aids in the continuing cycle of Ouroboros.

So I tell you as frater, as Parsifal, as Natas, reborn son of Babalon, the scarlet woman has been misunderstood and mistreated.

As Natas I do reject the Aeon of Horus and *The Book of the Law*. I embrace destiny and Thelema.

My disclaimer. Drink wine and take strange drugs. Who am I to judge, for I have partaken. It is true there are glimpses of illumination with chemical gnosis and that is fine. Using drugs to glimpse does not aid in the magician's growth much, though. Its weakness is to make one lazy. With dedication to the Great Work, illumination remains an option. Progress without drugs strengthens the abilities of the magician along the path of wisdom.

I deny *The Book of the Law* because it spawns a religion and for no other reason. I do not dispute the content. The days of religion have past. We are coming full circle.

So Babalon left me alone, feeling utterly empty, letting me observe myself. After having realized the lies being thrown at Babalon, I was unable to lie to myself any longer. I choose destiny.

Crowley was a genius, which was also his weakness.

No longer mistake the nature of the scarlet woman. She is much more than lustful sex and a whore. She is the force of creation and destruction. She destroys because it needs to be done.

Creation comes in more forms than simple organic copulation or the big bang. It is the act of creating everything, even the act of creating no thing. An artist's brush stroke. Sin is restriction, I agree, but sexual obsession is just another weakness which strengthens one when overcome. I say fuck 'til your heart's content and thoroughly enjoy the entire ride, yet give up the delusion that all that needs to be done is the fucking. Sex can become like drugs, a self-induced harness.

Weakness festers and grows when denied and ignored.

The scarlet woman is more than a cunt.

I'm going to have to come up with a method to point out the benefit of the proper method of work with the scarlet woman, the temple prostitute.

Destiny is free will, which is the reason it is difficult to grasp. Free will is the only thing able to grasp destiny.

The end of delusions.

With the Babalon Isis Working, Babalon did appear and let me continue to destroy myself. When the destruction is complete, the lies of the ego become clear. Your ego is ever-present and lurking about you.

I called Babalon to come and teach me and she did.

Having cried "Eureka!" again, I realize I am still lost.

Symbolic death and complete re-creation.

What I really know is that I know nothing.

"You asshole," a clean-shaven Frater Alpha spits at me. "You didn't work the Aethers. You didn't cross the Abyss. What kind of fucking idiot do you take me for? You're a fucking liar."

Instantly my anger peaks. An empty glass on the kitchen counter explodes.

"I don't lie."

Alpha's jaw drops, he takes a step back from me.

I look at the shards of glass on the counter and kitchen floor. "I didn't do that."

Frater Azazel rushes in from the other room. We are at his house. "Parsifal, Alpha, what happened?" He looks at the broken glass, the anger on my face, the pale of Alpha's face.

"I don't know," Frater Alpha says in a small voice.

Azazel's dark eyes accuse me. "She's waiting outside for you?"

"Who? Why did you invite me here? I thought the Golden Dawn forbade contact with me?"

"They have," Frater Azazel says in an annoyed tone. "We are with you today as initiates of a different order. Alpha resigned shortly after you did and joined me."

"What does this group want? What the fuck does everyone want?"

"You're the coal miner's canary," Alpha whispers.

Azazel answers, "The group knows nothing of you. You're the one who seeks. You choose to be chosen, as we all do."

I nod, looking down at the floor.

"Anasazi is outside waiting for you," Azazel says. "She's in the backyard."

I nod again and walk outside. I have know idea who Anasazi is.

It's still hot outside. A dirty, black summer. Gritty sweat and sunburns. The grass needs to be mowed.

In the backyard, an older, heavyset woman in a flowery sundress relaxes in a lawn chair, sipping lemonade and smoking a cigar.

"Have a seat," she says in a gravely voice as she motions to an empty lawn chair next to her. Her eyes are sharp.

I sit next to her in the lawn chair.

She introduces herself with an air of confidence. "I am Soror Anasazi."

I nod. "I'm Natas. You may call me Frater Parsifal."

She gives a hoarse laugh.

"Mm," she takes a puff of her cigar. "Look at that." She points to the street, visible from the open backyard. "Road kill."

I noticed it when I arrived, a bloody, gutty rabbit smashed nearly flat against the street pavement. I feel nothing and look back to her icy, blue eyes for explanation.

"Do you know a secret now?" She gives a Cheshire grin.

I clear my throat. "What secret?"

"Who is the lord of this world?"

"I don't know what you're talking about."

"You play that game often, Parsifal. Who is the one above the secret chiefs?"

My eyebrow raises. My feet shuffle. The summer heat dries my mouth. "Please speak more freely. Straightforward. I'm sick of mystery."

She cackles, rolling her head back.

I frown and fluster.

Her wrinkled hand brings the cigar to her mouth.

"Who are you?" I ask in a more forceful tone than intended. "Golden Dawn? Rose Cross? Silver Star? OTO?"

She blows smoke in my direction.

"The Silver Star," I curl my nose, "that's what I think."

She smiles. "Eager boy."

My shoulders slump. My body sinks into the lawn chair.

The old, plump woman continues in a soothing voice. "Who is the lord of this world?"

"I don't know."

"You do."

"I don't. I'm sorry to disappoint you."

"You lie to yourself and disappoint yourself, not me."

"I just haven't got the foggiest idea what you're talking about."

"It's right there before your eyes. You know the truth in your heart. You've known for some time. Let it out, boy. Vent it. Speak."

I stare at the dead rabbit. A hard, bloody corpse. Fear rises from my stomach and into my chest. My vision blurs. Tunnel vision focusing on the dead rabbit. I feel like leaving my body. Disassociation.

"Don't run from it, Parsifal. You've eaten from the Tree of Knowledge of Good and Evil."

I feel my lips move, almost unconsciously. "The morning star."

"What is the morning star?"

"The morning star and the evening star."

"Yes?" She rubs her hands together with glee.

"Yeshua ben Yosef," my voice quivers, "and all the ones they call Christ."

"The lord of this world?" she whispers.

I shake my head. "Lucifer."

She nods patiently.

"Lucifer," I continue, "is lord of this world. The renegade. The fallen archangel. The royal blood. A magician-king. A priest-king of Lucifer."

"Yes," she claps her hands together and chuckles, "Very good, my boy."

"Darkness pretends to be light. Lucifer is Prometheus. The bearer of light. The giver of fire to humankind. The adversary of the demiurge."

"And?" She smiles and sips her lemonade.

"Mary and Joseph are stations. Titles of priests. Magdalene, the scarlet woman of Jesus. High priestess, queen, temple whore, like Simon Magus and Helena, like Crowley and his scarlet women. Nicholas Flamel and Pernelle. They all followed the path of Lucifer, the angel who fights for humanity."

This gruff grandmotherly woman pats my hand, "Lucifer illuminates. Lucifer is the advocate of mankind. The Christian Church is the Black Brotherhood. The people, their slaves. Lucifer sets us free."

My shoulders straighten. "Lux Ferro. Lucifer is lord of this world."

She sits back and puffs her cigar. "It's an old spiritual war, Parsifal. From time to time things get out of balance, like during the second world war. The masses have been lied to. They are asleep. Sleeping sheep."

"I know," my tone surrendered.

"Parsifal," her voice solemn, "the Illuminati will not tolerate ronin."

"I understand."

"Do you? You're working emulated Jack Parsons' working to a slight degree. Your Black Pilgrimage is begun."

My eyes widen. "Can't I stop it?"

"No," her voice cracks, tears well in her eyes, "you've crossed the point of no return. What is done cannot be undone."

I nod.

"Take care, Parsifal," she shakes my hand, gripping it tightly in both of hers. "The Great White Brotherhood is watching, from everywhere."

She stands and hobbles away. Not into the house, but past the dead rabbit and down the street she disappears.

I must be ronin to survive this.

I go back into Azazel's house. Both magicians sit together playing video games.

I light a cigarette and watch, not sitting.

"What did she say," Azazel looks up from the game.

"Nothing."

"Nothing," Alpha says in a sarcastic tone.

"Who is she?" I ask.

"I don't know," Azazel shrugs. "She didn't say much. She said she is with an order. We talked and I believed her. She said she was here to recruit you since you resigned from the Golden Dawn. But I've never seen her before."

"You didn't think it strange?" I ask.

"Of course, we did," Alpha laughs, "but everything lately seems strange."

"When I talked with her, it was obvious that she is a higher ranking initiate than I," Azazel adds.

I nod. " I have to go."

In Jesod, Melissah and Sebastian appear to me. We are at the Temple of Pan with the angel Galabram.

"You've learned a little, canary," Melissah smiles.

Sebastian sits in silence.

Galabram appears slender, a faint blue tint to his skin. He reminds me of an ancient Egyptian. His clothes are loose and flowing.

Melissah continues, "You now know the 11:11 gateway. The pillars of the Tree of Life and the Temple of Jerusalem, Joachim and Boaz. Did you know it is also the thighs?"

I shake my head.

"Galabram," she continues, "please, tell us about yourself."

Galabram's voice is deep and melodic. "Close your eyes to see. Natas, we did live in Atlantis, as the people call it now. The language in which we communicate is easy and difficult. Atlantis will suffice. It is what it is known as today. Remembered as. We lived in Atlantis. A magician-priest. We fell with the other Atlanteans. A very few did not fall. Some walk the Earth. My name in Atlantis was Galabram. This other name, Benon, la cude vasey ireiku verus lax hoom, var zee bera kah… You must learn Enochian to speak my language. Angels are aliens. We are all the same. She wants you to change the world. You've felt this all your life. If you can see forward, you can see backward."

I scratch my head and curl my nose. "Um, is that supposed to mean something to me? Because I got to tell you all, I don't know how much more I can take. I feel like I've gone completely insane."

Sebastian sighs and waves a finger at me. "The Illuminati war has been going on since before the fall of Atlantis and has been fought by the same reincarnating souls. Many of them were high-ranking players during World War II, the United States' Revolutionary War, the Crusades of the Templar Knights, and ordeal of Jesus the

Christ and the birth of Christianity. The Roman Empire. Sumer. Just to state a few instances. It is happening now. You are a part of it. Why the hell can't you remember. We are star seeds!"

Melissah walks up to me and cups my chin in her hand, "Lucifer and Babalon were the first couple. Chokmah and Binah. Babalon is behind the formation of all mystical groups which have come from the Great White Lodge. The Secret Chiefs. Hillary is leaving you. Now wake up."

I wake mumbling, "Isis is Jesod."

Hillary and I cuddle on our green couch watching television together. My left hand caresses her cheek, looking in her eyes. "Don't worry, honey, it's all over now. I changed my mind about the whole thing. Don't be afraid. I can stop it all from happening. I made a stupid mistake. I thought I could have the best of both worlds. I love you too much to ever lose you. I can't live without you. I can't breathe without you. Everything's going to be alright."

Looking back into my eyes she replies, "I love you."

"I love you, too."

That night I dream of Babalon. She is walking down a staircase. I call out to her. She can't hear me. She walks out of sight.

I come home from work.

The Hillary comes out of the bedroom smiling at me.
I growl.

In her eyes are a tiny reflection of skulls and hourglasses.

"No," I choke out.

"Good-bye, Natas."

"No," I wail. "Please, God, no! I love you! Oh, no, no, no! Please, I love you. I love you. I love you so much!"

People look so beautiful as they walk out the door, as they walk out of your life. A mental photograph that haunts forever.

Lucifer looks so beautiful as he falls from Heaven.
Curled and crushed in a fetal position.
Defeated, deleted, and forlorn.
Sacrificed.

I'm bound in chains. Engulfed in the Black Odyssey coming. Alone. My wife, family and friends gone. My job gone. My home gone. My freedom gone. I've lost me somewhere in the Abyss. On my knees praying in Chapel Perilous. In Siege Perilous ferociously venerating. My love gone. My children gone. All material possessions gone. Everything I own gone. All gone. I'm stripped bare. Stripped naked. To the bones.

I die inside. Alone. Inescapable pain and misery.
Pain like I never fathomed could exist.

My entire being stripped of all its essence.
I die inside. Thrown into Hell. Devoured by the dogs.
Tortured and heckled. Beat. Alone. Hollow. My body grows frail and withers.
After 52 days the demons set me free.
Skinny and pale. Weak and lost. Alone and sore. Scabs on my head. I struggle to move and walk. All motivation dissipated.
Everything is gone. My life is gone.
Only the strong survive.
Even as ronin Illuminati I could not beat the will of the universe. I could not beat the Devil. The actions I set in

motion. I'll never fool myself again. I am not the man I was before.

My body, mind and soul regenerate.
Into something different.
I'm something different.
Something new.
A new man stands in the mirror forming.

I lay on a couch covered in sweat from the summer heat and my own dried tears.

My brother sits in a cushioned chair a few feet from me, sipping a bottle of beer.

My eyes open and close for a long period of time, half trying to sleep, but interested in the conversation my brother is having with me.

The tone of his voice sincere and concerned.

"Back when you were trying to get me involved in the magick with you, I had a dream about you. I dreamt I was a detective and your wife hired me to find you. When I started out I was investigating satanic metalheads and goths to find out where you went. I remember thinking, 'my brother would not have anything to do with these idiots.' As I went on searching deeper, the groups became more and more sophisticated. Like moving up a chain. More intelligent. More secret. Until I reached the level of people like Aleister Crowley and Timothy Leary. After reaching these types, I found you.

"When I found you I was shocked. When I found you, I found the Devil. With the classic goat head and hooves. The Devil spoke, *All paths lead to me.* The Devil didn't care about the dumb satan worshippers. He said they are easy prey. The real prize souls are guys like Crowley, Leary and you. Souls he has to work to get. People with intelligence present a challenge."

That night, I lay and grovel on all fours, weeping before the lord Lucifer.

Before me he stands tall and strong, a beauty too perfect to describe.

His silence absolute. Like the vacuum of endless space. He is the Statue of David come alive with almighty wings on His back.

I lift my wet face to meet His glorious gaze. My blue mortal eyes swallowed by his bluest immortal eyes. The horrific eyes of creation and oblivion.

My weak, quivering voice, "Please, let me go." I am a shivering mouse before the roar of a great lion.

His stoic eyes. No reaction.

"Please," the tears rage down my face. "I'm sorry. I know now. Now I know. I understand. When you left Heaven there was no greater pain. Infinite pain. Incomprehensible pain. Endless heartache. That's why you pull our souls down like gravity. Like a collapsed star. So we can feel the pain in the black hole of Hell. There will never be enough. It won't heal you. I feel your pain. Just a sliver of your pain and I can't survive it. I can't bear it. Please, let me go."

I cry on. "You have a way out. You always have. Unless you let me go, I will never be free. Heaven will forgive you one day. The pain will heal one day. I forgive you. You have my love. What more can you want? I'm at your mercy. I beg you, lord Lucifer, out of empathy, let me go. One day I'll be there, waiting for you to come home. Please, let me out of this pain. Out of your pain."

An eternal moment passes.

A single tear caresses the blue god's cheek.

The slightest nod.

My mouth falls wide open and smiles, tears of joy and freedom.

White feather wings sprout from my back, stretching boldly out.

With a single flap of wind, the white wings lift me off the ground.

I did not outsmart the Devil.

I understood the Devil.

Part Three

The Black Odyssey

"The Falls as a state of consciousness is analogous to that condition described by various mystics as the Dark Night of the Soul. It is accompanied by a sense of intolerable dryness, a dreaded awareness of the fact that all the powers of the soul seem dead, and the mind's vision closed in dumb protest, as it were, against the harsh discipline of the Work itself. A thousand and one seductions will tend to lure the candidate from the contemplation of the magical goal, and there will be presented to him a thousand and one means of breaking in spirit his vow to 'persevere in the divine science' without breaking it in letter. And it will appear that the mind itself will run riot and become unstable, warning the candidate that it were better for him to enjoy a lull in his magical operations."

— Israel Regardie, from the 1968 Introduction to *The Golden Dawn*

Fifty-two days later he rose again. My name is silence. Twenty-two silence for the great work.

———◆———

I live from intensity to intensity. One extreme to the next. I'm often confused by completion. Am I to preach the gospel of Babalon and the Aeon of Horus? No fucking way.

I now see the undercurrents which flow through life, just beneath the surface of history. Babalon gives me the Holy Grail. I thirst and the Grail over flows with the blood of life.

Her kisses on my lips. The moisture on my fingers. We press together against a wall. Our hands move over each other's bodies with graceful instinct and experience.

Her buttocks like a pale moon I grip with the hunger of the old ones. Her breast cupped in my hand, the soft nipple against my palm. My hard cock in her hand.

This spell was cast long ago with black clothe and candle wax. Semen buried in the dirt. Prayers and trance. It is a karmic debt from my last life. She wants me to hurt like she hurt. She died three years after I died.

To the outsider these confessions must seem like the ravings of the mad.

I run to return.

A love as strong as steel.

Babalon signaled her return with silent beauty and lust. I heard her call. Saw the machinations of Jesod.

I stand before you all, in all glory and shame, naked and whole. Alive and crying. Smiling, consumed with confidence.

Indigo child, son of a new age. A new soul and dawn. Establisher of the laws which are one.

The wider my eyes open, the more and less I see.

She knows me now. A best friend. A warm comfort. A game which is not a game.

When you're not here, I'd rather be alone. When you're not here, I'd rather have you come. When you're not here, I still hear your voice.

I'm standing in the parking lot outside the county jail at midnight. I just got out after serving 52 days in maximum security for aggravated assault. I thought I was going to prison until a week ago. I was looking at 30 years. Took a plea bargain and got time served with 6 months suspended and 3 years probation.

I had a rough time inside. A lot of guys gave me a hard time and threatened to fight me, thinking me a pussy because I was crying all the time. I have cried at least once a day for the past 52 days. My body has trembled and shaken with fear. But that's another tale entirely.

I tried to hang myself with white towels from an ugly green, paint-chipped railing. A cat from my cell block got me down before the guards found me. He woke me up, slapped my face and cussed at me in Spanish. He is a very cool cat. Mexican mafia. In for being an illegal alien. Said we can hook up on the street and pipeline dope up from Mexico together. Make big money. I told him I'm gonna walk the straight and narrow and try to save my marriage.

I haven't smoked in fifty-two days. The half pack of American Spirits in my hand is fifty-two days old. I take a stale cigarette out and look at it for a moment, thinking maybe I should quit. I've been through too much to do that. I need it to relieve some stress. Inhale relaxation.

I light the cigarette and continue standing in the empty parking lot, waiting on my friend. No moonlight tonight. Across the street I see the light of a gas station with some cat buying some beer inside.

I have three dollars in my pocket.

My friend should be here soon. I haven't seen him in a long while. I'm grateful that he's coming to get me and will let me stay at his house.

I lost thirty pounds while I was in jail.

Looking down at my old cowboy shirt, gray pants, and faded, red leather shoes, this seems so surreal. I can't wrap my mind around it. Fifty-two days ago my life changed forever.

I lost my job. My home was burglarized and everything I owned was taken. Everything. Computer. Television. PS2. DVDs. Swords. Comic book collection. My library. My clothes. All material possessions gone. Much worse, I lost my family. I even lost my dog and friends. Ha.

I lost her.

How could it have happened? I didn't see it coming. Life was normal, the day to day domestic thing, it seemed, and then BLAM, the universe slaps me silly and the magic carpet pulled out from beneath me.

Everything's gone.

I don't know what I'm going to do.

I love her so much. She has to come back. That love we shared, it couldn't have been a lie? How could she just shut herself off like that?

Sure we were getting a bit crazy and fighting. But the love was still there.

Damn it.

I told her I was a drug addict and an alcoholic. I told her I couldn't start partying again.

She was so disappointed that I'd failed as a writer. Urging me to succeed. Urging me to get back into the scene.

Fifty-two days ago I was about to be published.

What the fuck am I gonna do now?

I'm gonna stay clean now. Get a job. Earn her love back. Bring our family back together.

I'm gonna call her in the morning. Have to.

I can't sleep without dreaming her.

I can't get her out of my mind.

It was such a sweeping, whirlwind love affair. Wild, crazy love.

I love her.

Please come back to me.

Will you please come back to me, baby?

I've lost my marriage and my family. It hurts more than I ever imagined possible.

My wife says I need to learn how to love myself.

Headlights pull into the parking lot. It's my friend, driving a nice jeep. I feel a rush of calm.

Later that night, I lay on my friend's leather couch, in his living room, trying to sleep, tossing and turning. Where is she? Does she miss me? I'm sure once she hears my voice she'll remember us and everything will be fine. I'll be such a good man this time. A good man. A good father. A good husband. I'll do whatever she wants me to do. Whatever it takes. I'm committed.

I look at the digital alarm clock. It's three in the morning.

I pick up my friend's cell phone. Mine got shut off while I was in jail. I dial.

It takes several rings before someone answers.

"Hello?" The voice of my first ex-wife, sounding groggy.

"Kaley, I'm sorry for calling so late. I just can't sleep. I have to talk to Hillary and I don't have her phone number. I tried to call her but her phone is disconnected." I start to whimper and cry.

On the other end of the phone I hear Kaley sigh. "Don't ever call me this late again."

I can hear the anger rising in her voice. I beg, "Please, Kaley, I love her. I have to talk to her. Please, just give me her phone number."

"She doesn't want to talk to you."

"Please. I'll leave you alone after this, I swear."

"Hold on." There's a pause. "You're going to end up in jail again if you don't stay away from her."

"It'll be okay. I know it will."

Kaley gives me Hillary's phone number and hangs up.

I feel a constant sense of panic without Hillary.

Having her phone number gives me a sense of ease. Enough so that I drift into a restless sleep.

That morning I wake up at seven a.m. and pace the house, waiting for eight o'clock to come so I can call her. She'll have dropped the kids off at school at eight and I can call her and talk to her alone. My friend has already left for work.

At eight I dial the number, just a straight plunge. Nothing matters but her. I have to hear her voice. Fuck the consequences.

"Hello." Her voice makes my heart leap.

"Hillary?" My voice meek.

There is a long pause. "Hold on. I'll call you back." She hangs up the phone.

I sit on a black leather couch, staring at the dead phone in my palm. What the fuck? Back to jail?

Two minutes later the phone rings and I answer.

"You're out of jail? Why did you call me? I told Savannah I was going to call you. Why didn't you wait?"

"I couldn't wait. I can't take it. I need to know if you are divorcing me or not. I need closure. Something. Will you please come over and talk to me?"

A moment of silence. "That's fine. Meet me for breakfast. I'll buy."

We meet and eat. I have pancakes, French fries, and a cheese omelet. She has coffee, toast, and oatmeal.

"Jesus, Natas," she finally gasps after an awkward meal of small talk. "You look like shit. You're all pale and you have sores on your head. You're really skinny, too."

"Thanks. I didn't get much sun while I was in jail. The air was really dry in there, too. I didn't eat much food. I told them I was a vegetarian and they brought me a lot of peanut butter and jelly sandwiches, but I couldn't eat them because it reminded me of you packing my lunch for work every day. I didn't have much of an appetite for anything. I was getting fat anyways."

She laughs at me.

Not much else is said. Just more small talk. She gives me some money to buy cigarettes. "I just want to see you do good now. I want you to take care of yourself."

We go out to the parking lot. It's a nice, bright morning. I get in her car with her.

At first she lets me hug her and hold her hands and she is calling me honey and baby, but then she suddenly stops, pulling her small hands away from mine.

She says, "My mind is made up. We are divorcing and you just need to accept it."

"You're divorcing me?"

"Yes."

"Please, Hillary, don't do this. Just wait. Give me a chance to turn it around. Things just got fucked up. Just call it a trial separation. Just wait and watch me succeed. Watch me build things up like they used to be. Just wait and watch what I do. I can do it."

"I can't, Natas."

"Why not?"

She lights a menthol cigarette. "I'm just not the one for you. We're different people. I'm not going to let you manipulate me any more."

"Manipulate you? How did I manipulate you?"

"Like this. Talking with me and trying to convince me to come back to you. Making me think I still love you."

"I'm not manipulating you. Jesus. I'm just telling you the truth."

She laughs and smirks at me. "You need to go find yourself a good Christian girl who doesn't drink. Go be with Savanah. She loves you."

Tears well up in my eyes and quickly drip down my face and chin. "A Christian woman! What are you talking about? That's ridiculous. And I don't want Savannah, I want you."

"Natas, I'm done."

"No!" I cry and ball. My face is all wet with tears. "I love you so much. I love you with everything I have. How can you just let it all go?"

"It's not easy. I've already gone through my grieving while you were in jail. I cried for a month."

"Please, I love you." I drop my head into her lap and cry. My whole body shudders.

"Jesus," she giggles. "Just stop it. Quit crying. I have to go now. I have to go to Wal-mart. Alright. Enough."

I sit up and take a deep breath, wiping my eyes, "I'm sorry. I just can't live without you."

"You're just upset because you thought I couldn't make it without you."

"I never thought that. I know you're a strong person. I've always held you in the highest regard."

The whole time she is acting very peculiar, acting smug, like she is already over me and she isn't hurting at all.

"Well, I have to go."

"When do I get to see the kids?"

"I'll meet you at the park at one. They get out of school early today."

I climb out of her old, beat up car and watch her drive away from parking lot.

I'm going to succeed. I have to go find a job today. First project, I have to find my car.

One o'clock.

It's raining so she comes to my friend's house and hangs out for an hour. She's very closed off and won't make eye contact with me.

We're standing in the kitchen together. I say, "I'm glad that we are going to continue to be friends. I still need you as a part of my life, even if it's just as friends. I'll take what I can get."

She says, "I'll hang out with you once a week. On Sundays. But don't call me without permission."

"Okay."

"I don't have a problem with you seeing the kids. I know you're a good dad. You can see them once a week to start with."

I meekly nod. "Okay."

"I'm going to work out at the gym. The kids can stay with you until I get back."

"Thank you."

She leaves. The kids and I play video games and talk. Two hours later she comes back.

Looking all flushed from her work out, she walks in smiling at me. "Hi."

"Hey. How was it."

"Fine."

"Cool."

"Alright, Natas. Me and the kids will see you on Sunday."

My lips tighten and I nod. "Thank you so much. I can't wait."

"Oh, there's one more thing I've been thinking about."

"What's that?"

"I don't want you doing anymore magick."

"Why not?"

"I don't approve. It's why everything went so wrong. When I used to come home from work I could just feel it in the air. I could feel if you'd done a ritual that day or not. I think you brought something into our house. It scares me. If you want to see the kids or want me happy then no more magick."

I nod and whisper, "Okay."

Hillary gives me a hug after the kids do and they leave.

Two days later I come home and find a note on the door:

Natas,
I'm proud of you for getting a job! I can't allow you to hang out with the kids. This is what I believe is best. You are so manipulating. You will not do this to me anymore. I think it would be best if you try to contact a third party and explain your situation, that you want to see the kids. You will have to tell them so they can contact me. I'm not trying to hurt you...I just need to see you get better!
You are going in the right direction! Keep it up. You may send me letters in the mail to my mom's house.
If you call or come to either house I will call 911!

Love,
Hillary

I get a job working in a warehouse. Everyone there thinks I'm a lunatic because all I do is talk about my wife and kids, constantly. I spill my guts to perfect strangers, looking for advice. Looking for a solution, for help. Someone, please. I do my best to not think about magick, for Hillary. In truth I've become almost frightened of it.

Hillary calls me late one afternoon when I get off work and asks me to meet her at her mom's house. I'm so excited. I drive around waiting. Night falls and she calls again.

"Hello?"

"Hi, Natas. Meet me in the backyard. I don't want my mom to see you. Be quiet."

"Okay. Like a thief in the night, baby."

I park three blocks away. Walking to her mom's house I think about Aleister Crowley and some of his experiments with invisibility I read about. It's not actual physical invisibility, but more attempting to be incognito. To walk by people so discretely you are unnoticed. I do my best to emulate this behavior. Walking with stealth, silence and giving off the confidence that I belong right where I am, there is nothing out of the ordinary. The lights are on. I sneak into the backyard. It's dark. Almost black.

"Hey," she whispers from some bushes.

"What are you doing?" I whisper back with an amused grin at the sight of her hiding behind the bushes.

"Sh, just come here."

There is a patchwork quilt laid out on the grass, surrounded by bushes and trees. She's wearing my favorite sundress. "I always thought you were so beautiful in that dress."

"Thanks." She drapes her arms around my shoulders and kisses me. My eyes close and kiss her back.

We lay on the blanket and she lifts up her dress, wearing no panties underneath. We make love in the dark and when we're done she tells me to go away.

I walk back to my car feeling hopeful.

A couple of days later she calls me up and asks me to go to the park with her.

It's a hot, summer afternoon. We sit together on a park bench. A bright, colorful flower bed before us.

"Natas, I know you're not going to like this."

"What is it, just tell me." My heart sinks.

"I'm going to start seeing other people."

"No!" The tears I'm so used to now. "No, please, just wait. Just wait for me."

"I'm sorry."

I wrap my arms around her, sobbing. She lets me cry on her shoulder, patting me on the back.

Part of the Babalon Isis Working was to completely rip everything away from me. Fifty-two days of hell happened. Last summer I thought I was a slick Faust, could complete the working, and still have my wife and family. Over the last year I could feel them being tugged away. I performed the Working. I set the wheels in motion and thought I could stop it. Thought I could outsmart the devil. I changed my mind at the last minute when I came to my senses. I didn't want to lose my family and wife and everything to become. But it was too late. I wish I could go back in time and erase it all.

I see only one alternative now. One path. One way. To see this work through to its end. I have nothing left to lose.

I wake up. It's morning. Early morning. I'm used to waking up early, even though I'm not a morning person.

I'm living in my friend's basement now. On a sheetless mattress. I just lay there staring at the ceiling. I can't think of a reason to get up. I don't know how to stop hurting.

The basement isn't finished. It's cold, so I stay under the warmth of covers. There are spider webs between the ceiling studs. The floor is cold, concrete.

What's bothering me so much? It comes to me. The silence. I can't stand it.

I'm used to waking up to lots of noise and commotion. My wife running around the house like a busy bee. My children screaming and laughing and playing and watching cartoons. Everyone telling me to get up, we have things to do today.

I lie there and listen to this blank silence. This emptiness in the air.

I close my eyes and pull the blanket over my head. I just want to go back to sleep forever. I want to sleep my life away. Dreaming is so much better than being awake.

I feel sadness deep in my gut. Deep in my heart. In my throat. I could choke on it.

I just want to feel good again. I need to feel good. I need the pain to stop, or I'll go mad.

I think of Hillary.

I miss her so much. I think of her smell. The scent of her sneezes. Of her skin. Her hair. How she felt next to me in bed. The curves of her body. She was obsessed with being physically fit. Her stomach flat. Her muscles toned. Her cute, little, round nose and ass. Her laugh, a genuine bellow. I loved her laugh. Watching her paint while I would write. Drinking a glass of water every night before bed.

She would run a lot. At least twice a week. She would come home, all hot and sweaty, dressed in her silly, spandex running clothes. Tight clothes. A sports bra. It really turned me on. Kissing her while she was warm and her cheeks were flushed. Smelling her. Feeling, tasting her sweat.

I imagine her on top of me, making love like we used to. She would moan for me. We'd always find a perfect rhythm and a new adventure.

My hand reaches beneath my boxers. In my mind I'm there again. She's my wife again. She's panting that she loves me. I love you.

I don't mean to do it. It's a matter of reflex. Instinct. I am in a constant state of fight or flight. Imagining Hillary naked, floating above me in the akashic, transforms as we fuck. Her skin darkens. Her features elongate. She becomes this strange succubus I've met before. Floating in the astral light above me in the bed, she floats down and rides me. It's no longer Hillary. It's the amphibian woman with the vagina in her forehead. A third eye?

I fuck her with intent. Manifest. Please bring her back. My desire is too strong. That's the way magick works. If you wants something too much you'll never get it.

I whisper, "Come back to me. Come back to me, Hillary. I love you," as I cum.

The green woman whispers, "Reperio."

And I cry. Crushed with the guilt of the orgasm. I curl up like a baby and cry, but I've cried so much there are no tears left.

Parsifal served its purpose. I understand where I am. To a point. I had to become the sun to survive my spiritual death. I was the sun rising, climbing the day, setting. I somehow found the strength to navigate the underworld. The dead of winter. The death of the sun. Darkness before dawn. Now dawn is come and I am Saint Natas.

A few nights of drinking later I gather with some old friends from my new order, the *kult ov kaos*. We conduct a ritual. Alcohol, marijuana, amphetamines, and very, very strong LSD are consumed in honor of Nicholas Flamel's illumination. My conversion to Thelema is complete. Chaos magick. The belief system is my tool. The means to the end. The progress of the great work. The feeling I'm having is that my eyeballs are bleeding and screaming and my skull has flipped inside out. The spirit of Aleister Crowley appears in the room and chants the first two aethers. Everyone in the room is tripping balls. They have been asking about Crowley and we are all staring at a picture I drew of him and a photograph of him next to that.

I know the appearance of Crowley seems redundant. But he is here with us most of the time. Or at least that is the belief.

After a few days of recovery from the ritual I drive out into the country. It's a warm afternoon. Not hot, just right. I park my car and wander. An area of trees and trails I've designated my temple of Pan. Portions of the Babalon Isis Working were performed here. It's a very calm, secluded and green place. I feel at home here in this small forest. There is a friendly creek that trickles through the small wilderness.

I solemnly stroll to the creek's edge. In my hands are a black double-cubed altar, my ritual dagger, wand, cup and pentacle. I set them in the flowing water and watch them float away for a moment before I walk away. I don't need these devices any longer.

I walk back into the trees. Finding the oldest big tree I can and I take out a knife, cutting away a circular area of bark. I perform the Lesser Banishing Ritual of the Pentagram. In the bald patch of the tree I carve a sigil. I lay out an offering of food and tobacco. Praying on my knees. The lotus working is performed. The sigil charged. I cover the sigil with nectar, perform the LBRP a second time, and declare the ritual closed.

I am now living Thelema. I have accepted the law. Thelema in action is a bit frightening at times. Sometimes taking leaps of faith. Listening to that guiding inner voice whispering True Will. It's tedious to maintain and stay grounded in the mundane world of a consensus reality. I could very easily turn my back on society as a whole, but having done so in the past I found it to be very unproductive beyond my own pleasures.

Now the goal is to spread Thelema as far and wide as my words carry. Having a natural rebellious streak it's hard for me to accept that Crowley was a prophet of an Aeon. It's a thin line between the philosophy of the Crowley-ite and the Thelemite. An inner compass guides the Thelemite. The words and legend of Aleister guide the Crowley-ite. Really, I'm neither. Call it Thelema. Call it my will. I am my own man.

I don't like to speak in specifics when discussing my True Will. In my experience there is power in silence.

Magick dew seems to roll off the tongue much smoother with quiet intentions.

And I don't know where we are all going. These words I write, these words I will, these words are invocations. I feel the earth move under my feet. I feel the sky crumbling down, crumbling down. I feel the earth move under my feet. I feel the sky tumbling down, tumbling down.

Ah…da fone doth reeng.

High on a hill with a lonely goat…lay eho lay eho oh yo da lay yo da lay yo da lay eho lay da.

We invoke white trash goddesses. Gods of sex, drugs and rock and roll. Angels of hip hop.

Oh, the phone, the night just called. Gotta split. Celebrate Pan and Dionysius. Drink wine and take strange drugs.

Do what thou wilt.

I've quit couch surfing and moved into my own apartment. I sit on the living room couch. An old orange and tan flowered couch I got for free. It looks like it was made in 1974. When I moved in here it was nothing but myself, a garbage bag of clothes, a pillow, and a sleeping bag. Now I have a disco globe hanging from the living room ceiling. I've come a long way since my last jail stint. Ha.

I sit alone on this old, soft couch, rolling a joint on a coffee table I bought for five dollars at the Salvation Army. I use the Zig Zag pack to comb the seeds and stems out of my weed. Back and forth, back and forth I sift the seeds out. They roll to one side of the paper plate. I use a cigarette roller to make my joints.

Taking a hit, I look at my black and white leather wallet sitting on the coffee table. I'm almost out of money. It's going to be a long stretch until next payday. The pot cost me a good chunk of money, scrape by.

I've been hanging out with Jackie and Savannah most every day. We just talk, drink wine, and smoke cigarettes all day, every day. We've been going like this for a few months.

Savannah's been complaining about me smoking weed. She said, "I thought you said you were only going to drink? No drugs? Come on, Natas, you're boring when you get stoned. All you do is sit there and stare at the TV. You don't talk to me as much anymore." She's been my best friend for years.

On the other hand, Jackie is fine with the weed smoking. She used to be a pothead back when we were young, too. I'm just returning to my roots, is all. I've turned her back onto it a bit.

I've been pretty excited the past few weeks because Savannah's best girlfriend, Serenity, is showing some interest in me. She is smoking hot. Long black hair, full lips, curves in all the right places. She just oozes sexuality. She dresses like a sex kitten. Like a pussycat. Promiscuous. Terrible to say that. I do like her a bit. Well, I know she's so hot that a lot of other guys want to get with her, but she's with me now. And I can't help but like it even more because it seems to make Hillary act jealous. Hillary says Serenity is fat, which is utter bullshit. They had a slight, awkward confrontation the other day. I wasn't there. Got it second hand from both of them.

I've been eating acid and mushrooms. Doing coke and meth. Smoking weed and drinking every day. I can't afford it anymore.

Jesus, a week or so ago I left the bar and went to an after bar party. I was all drunked up. Fucking wasted. These bar folk I barely remember went to the basement to party. There was some fat chick with huge tits down there lying in a bed. I don't really know who the people were I was with. Still don't. I got them all stoned. We went back upstairs because the fat chick said she was going to sleep. I wandered around the house a bit. Didn't really care to talk to the hipsters sitting in the upstairs living room. Couple of them just want to kiss my ass so I'll smoke more pot with them. Really it's getting old. All these god damned fucking hipsters and scene-sters. Local artists. Painters and writers. Musicians. Tattoo artists. Film makers. Rappers. Poets. Activists. Whatever. People dressing all hip and cool, like wanna-be rock stars. The "in" crowd. Acting like they're in high school. Elitist cool kids, but none of them are kids anymore.

They're too fucking dry, too sweet, whichever way you cut it. Mostly a bunch of yuppie fuckers, pretending to be starving artists. All indie. None of them grew up in the dirt. They emulate the down and dirty renegades, but when confronted by the real down and dirty renegades they wet their pants.

Fuck it. Fuck 'em all.

I wander back downstairs to the fat chick with the big tits. Jesus, each of her tits is the size of my head. These are true melons.

"Hey," she smiles from bed as I stand, holding onto the door frame, swaying at the foot of the stairs.

"Hey," I slur and stumble toward her.

She's talking to me, I have no idea about what. Something about college and her friends at school. Do I want to go to a play with her next weekend? I just walk

Confessions of a Black Magician

straight to her bed and start kissing her mid-sentence. She seems shocked but kisses me back hard. I kiss her all over. None of these hipster fuckers would lay a finger on her. She's not hip enough. Not beautiful enough. I am.

Doesn't take long until I'm in the bed, mounting her, both naked and fucking hard. I can't believe the weight of her tit in my gripping hand. I can't believe it. I've never felt tits this big before. I become completely lost in indulgence, burying my head between her breasts. She rubs them all over my body. It feels nice.

We fuck in every position I can think of. I pound her pussy hard with my cock. She's screaming loud in delight. The headboard is beating against the wall. All the hipsters upstairs have to go outside and drink in the front yard to get away from our yelling and fucking frenzy. I become a complete beast chanting "IO! IO Pan!" We have sex for about two hours. Drenched in sweat and panting.

We pass out. I wake up a few hours later to her sleeping naked next to me. The blankets are on the floor. I sit in awe at the size of her tits, lying there, huge mounds of soft, round flesh in the morning window sunlight.

I sneak out of the house before she wakes up. I never talk to her again. When I see her at the bar I pretend I don't know who she is. I do tell my "friends" about the incident. Another night at the bar, a few months from now, one of the guys from that party sees me and says, "You're treacherous, Natas," and walks away from me when I tell him, "I got no grass, jack." His statement sums up the reputation I'm stepping into.

I start doing that a lot. Just sleeping with every woman that wants to sleep with me. I just don't care. I'm lonely and don't want to hurt anymore. I let whoever wants me, have me. I fuck them and then ignore them. Moving on to the next fix.

But this morning Serenity and I woke up next to each other again. We spent the late morning hours in bed, talking, cuddling, drinking water, smoking cigarettes. A familiar scene now. We've spent a few nights together.

I tell her I like her a lot. Inside I'm hoping we fall in love and take it all the way. I think, I could commit to her. I'll be loyal and good and honest and treat her like an angel. I'll take care of her. Give her whatever it is she wants.

So I tell her I like her.

She says she likes me, too. She likes me, too, but...

She tells me she wants to take things slow. She says she's afraid to be vulnerable. She doesn't want to get hurt. She says, "I was watching this interview on TV with the actor, Colin Farrell. He was talking about why he isn't with anyone. Why he doesn't have a girlfriend. He said he doesn't feel it would be fair to expose someone else to him, because he is so fucked up. So he just chooses to be alone. It went something like that. I really liked that. It's how I feel. I just couldn't put it in words before."

I nod. "I like it. That's cool." I realize how much sense that makes. I shouldn't expose anyone to my madness either.

I don't ever try to call her again. We see less and less of each other. In the near future she will hear about another and me and question me over the phone. "I thought you were just friends? That you didn't like her like that?" I can hear a tiny sorrow in her voice. We never speak or see each other again.

Coming out of this daydreaming, this reminiscing, my joint is half gone. I feel so relaxed and happy. Music sounds so good. I've scribbled a poem on a piece of paper on the coffee table.

I look at my empty wallet again. Thinking. Thinking.

I know enough people that like to smoke weed. Jackie would probably buy it from me regularly. Let's see. If I just get enough to sell to about six people, I will make enough money to pay for my own marijuana habit. I won't have to tap into my paychecks to buy marijuana anymore.

I put the joint out and set the roach on the door ledge between my living room and bedroom.

I light a cigarette and start to dance around the living room. My bare feet against the wood floor, and I sing, quietly, "Don't you remember you told me you love me baby, you said you'd be coming back this way again baby…baby, baby, baby, baby, oh baby, I love you…I really do."

I smile, take a drag off my cigarette, pull my phone out of my pocket. "Joss, hey man, what's happening? I gotta talk to you about something, but I don't wanna talk about it on the phone."

A little later I walk into Joss' house feeling a bit out of my element. When I was younger I would go to drug houses all the time. The fact that it's a drug house doesn't bother me in the slightest. That what I'm here for. And I like most of these guys. This can't be considered a complete drug house, in the street level sense, it's not a house of crackheads or junkies. This is a party house for youth just out of high school and in early college who do a lot of drugs. This is what makes me feel uncomfortable and out of place. I am 32 years old. Everyone in this house ranges from age 17 to 21. Culture tells me I'm supposed to hang out with people my own age.

I walk in to this small, dirty house. High school kids and college kids sit around the living room playing 'Halo', listening to music, smoking cigarettes, passing bowls, and drinking beer. I get curious looks from the ones who don't know who I am. Expressions like, who is this old dude?

Before I can say anything after walking in, Byron walks in the room with a big grin, his long blond curls bouncing, his eyes bloodshot. "Natas! Oh, man, this is so fucking awesome. I'm so glad you're here, man! You're the coolest motherfucker in town. Come here, gimme some love." My jolly friend gives me a tight hug and pats me on the back. "What have you been up to, man?"

I shrug. "Nothing. Just hanging out. Working. Gettin' drunk. Gettin' stoned."

He laughs. "Hell yeah!"

I take a seat next to Byron on the floor and look around the room. There is the quiet Snoop in his glasses and sandy blond afro; Henry a happy, farm boy and gear-head drunk who everyone loves; Erik the long haired, intellectual, punk rock lady killer; Abner, Joss' quiet younger brother; and Jim, the cockiest, good looking, spoiled rich kid anyone ever met. There are also a bunch of girls buzzing around that I don't know. A few other cats, too.

Joss comes out of his bedroom with a serious expression, looking like a drugged-out hippie version of Tom Cruise. "Natas, Byron. Come in here." He sounds all dramatic and serious. Abner tries to follow with one of his younger friends. "No, Abner," Joss says. "We have some business to take care of."

The bedroom is tiny, hardly room to walk around the bed and dresser. Joss pulls several pounds of marijuana out of his beat up dresser. "How much you want?"

"I don't know," I shrug. Byron hands me a pipe and I take a long hit. "I don't have any money. I wanted to know if you'd front me?"

Byron is laughing. "Dude, Natas, dude, you have to check this out," he opens the closet door.

I step over dirty clothes and look in. There are five potted marijuana plants and lights to help them grow. "Nice," I nod, "Very fucking nice, man."

Joss says with pride, "Each one is grown from different dank seeds. It's going to be killer. I can't believe how big they are already."

"Yeh, very cool." I take another hit of weed and hand the pipe to Byron.

"So how much did you want, Natas?" Joss asks fiddling with his black electronic scale on the dresser.

"Well, like I said, I haven't got any money today."

"Natas," Byron spouts with his usually jolly animation, "We love you, man. We know we can trust you. Me and Joss have been talking about it and we want you to start selling with us."

I nod.

Joss lights a cigarette and sets his beer on the dresser next to a pile of fluorescent green marijuana buds and his scale. "You've been getting a lot of weed from us. As long as you can sell it, I'll front you as much as you want."

"I don't know, man," I answer. "That's cool. I just don't know how fast I can move it."

"Shit, Natas," Byron chuckles and puts his hand on my shoulder. "That first night we hung out you said you didn't smoke weed anymore! Now look at you. You were right.

You said if you started smoking again you would go all out."

"Yeh," I smile, "I'm glad I started tokin' again."

"You rock, man," Byron grins. "Wanna get drunk with us tonight? Come on! Let's get some Mickey's!"

I shake my head, "I have to work in the morning, but I got this bird coming up to buy an ounce from me tomorrow. She's actually like driving five hours to get it from me. Her and her husband come up and buy an ounce off me about once a month. I'm just dry. My Mexican's dry. That doesn't happen often. I can't keep up with what people wanna buy from me and I ain't got no money now."

"Natas, Natas, man." Byron has his arm around me. "I told you, man, we're brothers, you, me and Joss."

"Yeh, I know, man. I love you guys."

Joss starts talking to someone on his cell phone.

"How about if we give you a pound," Joss suggests.

"Holy shit," I smile, "That's fine with me. I'll see what I can do with it."

"I just need some money tomorrow," he adds.

"I told you that couple's coming for an O.Z."

"We know you're good for it," Byron smiles.

These guys are my friends. I've known them all for a couple of years and always liked them. We just never hung out because of our age difference, I guess. Fuck it. Fuck the rules of society and cultural. I'm here to break all taboos. Do what thou wilt.

Joss weighs out a pound and wraps it in plastic wrap. I stick it under my shirt and inside the waist of my pants.

"Alright, man," I say. "Thanks for the front. I gotta split."

"I fucking love that shirt man," Byron says. "You're the coolest fucker, Natas."

I look down at the shirt. It's a long sleeved white button-up shirt with a big, black jolly roger stitched in the front of it. I put my black hooded sweatshirt back on and zip it up.

As I leave, everyone says good-bye to me and a few shake my hand.

Jim follows me outside. We sit in my car and smoke a joint together. He tells me that I'm selling weed faster than Byron and Joss can and I should be their full partner. I'm a little surprised at how fast I can sell the weed. I guess once I dove back into it I knew way more people than I thought.

There is nothing double handed going on here. Nothing like that. I've been partying with these guys more and more over the past month and spending less time with the old crew of Savannah, Jackie, Serenity, and their bunch of late twenties/early thirties barfly hipsters. My friendship with Joss, Byron and Jim has actually been building serious tension between Savannah and me. She refuses to hang out with Joss, Byron, Jim or any of their friends anymore. Ever since we took Joss to a bar where these birds were dancing with their shirts off on the bar and I told Joss to get up there and dance with them. He did. If I was younger I would've, too. The bartender got mad and pushed Joss off the bar. He fell and knocked over a bunch of big jock-like motherfuckers beers. They were going to beat me and Joss up and we were out-numbered. Savannah and her friends were too sweet to fight, so Joss and I ended up paying for the beers. Savannah says it's wrong for me to hang out with people so much younger than me. She's really pissed I'm selling drugs now, too. For me selling the drugs is like fuck it or fight it, it's all the same. For me selling drugs is my one-man revolution. My big "fuck you" to the system.

Jim and I make plans to hang out this weekend and then I go home.

The drive home makes me so nervous. Every time I'm driving around with a lot of weed I get paranoid of cops. I have enough on me to put me in prison. Fuck, it's nerve racking. I do my best to drive as inconspicuously as possible.

I evoke an entity I've named the dream witch. I call it to see what happens. She slips in the dreaming through Jesod. Be lucid. Hear with your ears. See with your eyes. Don't believe. Inquire.

She is in possession of *The Necronomicon*. The tome is in the akashic, in her home. The akashic unconsciously accessed by H.P. Lovecraft to reveal snippets of this dreadful grimoire. H.P. Lovecraft knew this book by the title, *The Necronomicon*. Aleister Crowley knew it by another name. John Dee by another name still. It is one book in a collection, so to speak. But who dares to read and scribe *The Necronomicon*?

The dream witch is coming for you 23. It begins March 1. A day of the witch trials in Salem, 1692. 1932 the Lindbergh baby is kidnapped. 1949 *Ripley's Believe It Or Not* debuts. 1974 seven are indicted in the Watergate scandal. 1994 *Nirvana* plays their last show in Munich, Germany. March 1 is the day to observe the sacred fire of Rome renewed. Two days from the full moon and in a blizzard. Her number is 278. Fear not, she is an exterminating angel.

I've been up drinking and doing lines of cocaine all night with Eva, her fiancé, Rodney and Savannah. Rodney and Savannah are passed out naked in Savannah's bed next door.

Eva and I are sitting on my bed, passing a half empty bottle of Jack Daniels back and forth, finishing up the coke, and watching the sun rise through the window.

She's beautiful. Dark eyes, long brown hair, slender, curvy, a deep, sexy voice. Her nostrils are red from the coke. Her eyes are bloodshot from the Jack. She's topless. Her bra and shirt lay on my floor. We've already made love. She doesn't really have romantic interest in me. My wallet isn't thick enough. She's just getting revenge for Savannah and Rodney sleeping together. I don't care. It's not the first time we've been together. She's stunning. She could be a model or some kind of celebrity.

"I can't believe those fuckers did that to me. I mean Savannah's been my best fucking friend since high school and Rodney's been with me for years." She shakes her head, her breasts shake.

"I don't know what to tell you, it sucks." We've all known each other since high school.

Eva lays her head on my shoulder and hands me the bottle.

I take a shot and almost gag. "Hillary's going to be here soon."

"Why's she coming over?"

"To drop off my son."

"I've never met her," Eva mumbles.

"Yeah, it really kinda sucks. I'm really heartbroken over her."

"Savannah told me, but from what Savannah and everyone's told me, I don't understand why you like Hillary at all."

"I don't know. I guess everyone meets their match eventually."

"You need to forget about her and find someone new."

My hand reaches out and plays with Eva's breast. My thumb strokes her nipple.

"Mm," she smiles.

There is a knock at the door.

"Shit," I kiss Eva on the cheek. "She's here."

"What should I do?" Eva's eyes widen. "I feel all uncomfortable. I don't want to see her."

"Come out and make her jealous." I giggle and stand up.

"No fucking way," Eva growls.

I walk out into the living room and shut the bedroom door, then walk into the kitchen and answer the door.

The tiny, blonde, spitfire, Hillary, stands before me holding a bag of clothes. My toddler son stands at her side, holding a toy car.

My heart thumps. I stand swaying and grinning in the doorway. "Hey!"

"Jesus, have you been drinking?" Her eyebrows angle.

"A little bit."

"Is our son going to be okay with you or do you need to pass out?"

Smiling, I shake my head. "He'll be fine. We'll be fine. I'm fine. Just tired."

"Okay," she sighs, setting the bag down.

My boy puts the toy car down on the floor and wanders into the living room.

"So can I have a hug?" I smile and stagger a bit.

"No," she chuckles.

"I heard you have another boyfriend now."

"Where'd you here that?"

"Word on the street," I shrug.

"Well, so what, I heard you're seeing that slut Serenity."

"Slut? Come on, baby, she's a nice girl. But I'm not seeing her anymore, if I ever was."

"Duh, she looks like a bar skank."

"I don't think so. I think she's sexy as hell."

"Jesus, she's a fucking whore."

"Who's yer new man?"

"That's none of your business."

"Is it Roach?"

She just looks at me.

"Holy fucking shit! It is Roach! That piece of fucking shit asshole! I knew it! I knew you were cheating on me!"

"Oh fuck you. I wasn't cheating on you, but if we would've stayed together any longer I would have!"

"Don't lie! I knew that first night you came home after meeting him, all excited, babbling on about how the punk rockers finally accepted you! Fuck. That was high school for me, baby."

"Fuck off mister fucking badass too cool fuckhead."

"You had an affair with Roach!"

"So what if I did?" she yells at me.

"Ah! Fuck!" I raise my arms up over my head, hands gripping my head.

"Oh, just calm down, Natas. You have to behave for our son now. Let me hug you." She reaches for me.

"Get the fuck away from me!" I scream and push her back. She falls, landing on one knee.

In a fit of rage I reach out for the first things I see and destroy. A row of wine glasses on the kitchen counter, my hand sweeps out and knocks them all over. They shatter into the sink and across the counter.

My son's brand new toy car on the floor at our feet. I raise my foot and smash it.

My son runs into the room. "Daddy," he's visibly upset, "You broke my car!"

"Oh, God," my voice a sudden whimper, my hands cover my mouth. "I'm so sorry."

"Come on." Hillary takes his little hand. "Let's go." She glares at me. "I'm so tired of this shit. You're fucking insane. You're lucky I don't call the cops." She slams the door.

I can hear early morning birds chirping outside.

I fall to the floor and sit there, staring at my son's smashed car.

What the fuck did I do? I'm out of fucking control.

"What was that all about?" Eva is standing in the kitchen doorway, topless with the bottle of Jack in one hand, a cigarette in the other.

"Just leave," I answer in a quiet tone.

"Oh, come here, baby." She drops to her knees next to me and drapes her wrists over my shoulders. Her forehead rests against mine. "It'll be okay."

"No, it won't." Tears race down my cheeks.

"Oh, oh, baby, don't cry." She kisses me on the lips and wipes away tears.

I kiss her back. I pick her up, still kissing, and take her to my couch. She unbuttons my pants and starts to stroke my cock. I kiss and fondle her breasts.

"No." I pull back. "No, no, no," I stand up, shaking my head and pulling my pants back on. "I have to go and make this right."

Eva cackles in her hoarse voice, "Don't be a fucking idiot."

"I have to go. I fucked up."

She shrugs. "Fine. Fuck off."

I look at her a moment and shrug inside. Then I walk out the door.

I pull up in front of Hillary's house.

Roach is standing on the porch smoking a cigarette.

Fuck, I think, just ignore the bastard. He can have her.

I walk up the front stairs of her house, and walk past him as he glares at me, I walk into the house and up to her apartment door.

Knocking.

"What do you want, Natas?" She doesn't open the door.

"I just want to say I'm sorry."

"You're always sorry."

"I know. I'm sorry."

"Just go."

"When can I see our son?"

"Tomorrow, when you're sober."

"Okay," I nod. "Okay. I'm going now."

I walk down the stairs and outside onto the front porch with Roach standing there smoking a cigarette.

I look at him, all skinny and arrogant. Dreadlocks, black metal t-shirt, ripped pants, leather jacket, tattoos. He mad dogs me.

I stop and start to pull out a cigarette of my own. "So did you have an affair with my wife?"

"So what if I did?" he smiles. "What are you going to do about it."

I put the cigarette back in its pack as I respond, "I'm going to kick your fucking ass right now."

"Come on!" he yells at me, eyes enraged.

I swing. My fist connects with his forehead. My other fist swings and hits his jaw.

My arms flurry, hitting him in the head several times.

He wraps his arms around me, grabbing my hooded sweatshirt. He tugs it completely over my head, blinding me.

I stop swinging and charge forward with all my strength.

The momentum of me crashing into him sends us both flipping over the porch railing onto the ground.

I keep hitting him and hitting him in the face.

With one hand I hold his dreadlocks, holding his head down on the ground, pounding his face with my other fist. I hit him again and again. Thud. Thud. Thud. I want blood.

I look down at him and see defeat and fear in his eyes.

A tinge of guilt seizes me. Still holding him down by his dreadlocks, I say, "I'm going to let you up now. I'm going to let you up as long as you don't hit me. Just let me leave now."

"Okay," he says quietly.

I step away from him. "I'm sorry. I'm sorry I beat you up. You shouldn't have fucked my wife."

"You should have treated her better," he groans on the ground.

I get in my car and drive away.

I drive to my older son's house.

He gets in the car with me and we drive around.

I'm crying. "I'm sorry." I hug him. "I just beat some guy up."

Hillary texts me saying she's called the police.

"The police are looking for me. I'm sorry. I'll take you home."

He hugs me. I see the concern in his eyes. "Are you going to jail again?"

"I don't know. Don't worry. I'll figure it all out. Everything will be okay. I love you so much. Don't be scared, okay?"

"Okay," he nods and I take him back home, realizing I shouldn't be driving around drunk with my son. Realizing I better stay away from my sons to protect them from me.

I hug him good-bye and tell him I'll call him later and he and his brother and I will all hang out.

I drive around sweating and smoking cigarettes. I've turned into a monster. I can't go home. The cops are looking for me. I have to hide out somewhere.

I drive over to Joss' house. He's the only one home.

I sit on his couch and start crying again.

"Whoa, whoa, what's wrong?" He throws his arms around me. "You're okay."

I nod and tell him about the fight with Roach.

"Well, you can stay here. I have to go to work right now, but you can stay here as long as you want." He just got a job as a server at a Sushi restaurant.

"Thanks, man." I light another cigarette. "Got any weed for me to smoke? I need to mellow out, feel all strung out from the coke and Jack."

"No problem." He pulls out a purple, glass pipe and we smoke a bowl.

After he leaves for work I sit on his couch trying to watch TV.

"Fuck," I shake my head and leave. I don't want to be alone.

I drive aimlessly around town. What the fuck am I going to do now? I can't believe I've fucked up again. A light bulb goes off. I drive over to Gray's house. His girlfriend lets me in. He's hung over and in bed watching TV.

I sit on the bed next to him and start crying again, telling him everything that happened.

"You can sit here as long as you want," he says, looking a bit concerned and bewildered.

"Got a phone book?"

He gives me a phone book. I start looking up phone numbers for rehab centers.

"Hello?"

"I need to get into treatment."

"Do you have insurance?"

"No."

They go through several questions with me telling me I have to come in on Monday for a chemical dependency assessment.

I dial another number.

"Natas, what's up?" a cheery voice asks.

"Francis, I need help." I cry.

Gray continues sitting next to me watching TV. He looks at me with empathy and confusion spread over his face.

"What's wrong?" Francis asks, his voice filled with genuine concern.

"I fucked up. I relapsed. I'm drunk and on drugs. I beat up Hillary's boyfriend and the police are looking for me."

Francis and I make plans to hang out. He says he'll help me any way he can. I've known him for years. I helped him get sober when he was younger. He's a very good person. A strong Catholic. A musician and a member of Alcoholics Anonymous. He's a good friend, always there for me.

I make several phone calls. All phone calls to rehab centers. I know I'm out of control.

I leave Gray's house that evening at dusk.

I don't follow through with any of the plans I made on the phone with Francis and rehab.

Another night.

I sit watching my television alone in the dark. Always smoking a cigarette. Everyone else has passed out or gone to sleep. A mellow night. I seem to have more friends now than I know what to do with. It doesn't fucking matter. The money in my pocket doesn't matter. I can't bring myself to care about anything. I just don't give a fuck. I've always rebelled, but this is something else entirely. The ultimate rebellion. Rebellion against everyone and everything. Rebellion against the rebels. Rebellion against love and hate. Rebellion against culture and everything around me.

My life ended with the Babalon Isis Working.

I just want to go to sleep forever. I want to sleep and never wake up. I really want to just die. I'm tired. Life has beat me up so much. I just can't do it anymore. God. I'm too afraid to kill myself.

Why? Why not. Fuck it. Just do it.

But how?

I'll overdose. I'll just party until I overdose.

If I had a gun...

Jesus, I don't want to end up like that one guy who tried to kill himself after Kurt Cobain died. Shot himself in the face with a shotgun and lived. Horribly scarred. He blew his face off and lived. Had to live his life looking like the Elephant Man.

If I had a gun I'd do it right now.

Really, I just want to die.

I feel a choke in my throat. My eyes get warm.

I watch the cigarette smoke dance upward from the ashtray, illuminated by the television light. The shadows bounce and hop around the walls.

Razor blades to my wrists? I could slice my wrists in the bathtub, get good and drunk and high and pass out while I bleed to death. Listening to music. I wonder what song I should listen to?

It's a late night talk show on the television screen. I have the volume on mute.

I could just smoke this joint and stay high forever.

"Natas," a quiet voice says from the darkness.

Standing in the door way of a bedroom I see the shape of Luba in the shadows.

"Um, yeah?"

"Can I come out and join you?"

"Sure." I shrug and put my cigarette out.

"Are you okay?"

"Hmm? Yeah. What do you mean?"

"Are you going to kill yourself?"

I freeze. What? What? How could she know that? What the fuck? Who is this bird?

"What are you talking about?" I try to hide my shock with a cocky smirk.

She shrugs.

I look at the funny shape of her lips. Her long, cute nose. Her hazel eyes. Brown hair.

Her voice is usually crass and loud, obnoxious, but now her voice is soft and truly caring. "I've been watching you. I can tell that you're really sad. I just thought that maybe you were thinking about killing yourself."

I tilt my head to the side and shake it. "No, no, of course not."

"Okay," she almost whispers and looks at the television screen. David Letterman is on the screen grinning about something.

I press my hands flat against my face and rub. I rub my eyes, and run my hands through my short hair. "You can tell I'm sad?"

She nods, a silhouette in the doorway.

"It's hard to talk about. I guess I'm a little sad."

"I know."

"That's crazy. All these people around me and none of them notice."

"They all think you're mister cool drug dealer. Mister party animal. High roller."

"I guess."

"Everyone likes you, Natas. Why are you so sad?"

"I don't know. I guess I'm just heartbroken. Just tired and feeling beat up by life. Just tired of it all."

"Who broke your heart?"

"My wife left me. Jesus. I shouldn't be talking to you about this. How old are you anyways?"

"Seventeen."

"Fuck," I shake my head. "What am I doing hanging out with you?"

"Who cares about age? It's just a number."

I look into her big hazel eyes.

She silently walks over and sits on the couch with me. We just sit, looking at each other.

I look down at the wood floor. "I'm pretty fucking sad."

"I know," she whispers. Her soft hand takes mine. I watch my tear fall onto the back of her hand. "It's okay now," she whispers, "I'm here now."

The days seem to blur into each other.

My car died today. It died because I never changed the oil. I left work yesterday and went to the doctor. They think I have a slipped disk. I just didn't want to work. It's warm out. I bought three *Fraggle Rock* DVDs yesterday. A local punk rock venue asked me to become involved, help book shows and what not. I said, "Sure, why not?" I sleep with a baseball bat and carry a can of mace in my pocket. Nunchaku at my side when I'm at the computer. At the doctor's office they wanted to stick me in rehab. I said, "No, I'm cool." I've very much embedded myself in the criminal element and am fully exploring it. I have a bunch of friends and a few birds, but feel very much alone every day.

Financially I am very poor. I grew up dirt poor. Born in the gutter. Day to day I just let things roll the way they roll. I'll be taking a trip to Colorado soon. The happiest moments in my life right now are when my sons are with me. I very much miss being a full time father.

What I like about magick is the experience. What you actually did and what happened. What omens/signs/synchronicities did you see? What did that praeterhuman intelligence have to say? How do we stay illuminated and continue to function effectively in sleeping societies?

I've started studying Nietzsche again. A jack of all trades, master of none, if I am, layman scholar of Crowley,

Jung and Nietzsche. I am a posthumous hero. My words/time-bombs stretch further than my current vehicle's linear perception.

My life is not my own. I am tiny particles flowing in a cosmic river. Trickling quietly until I am dispersed in the great ocean at the end of everything.

───◆───

I'm falling asleep, naked on my old, orange-flowered couch. Didn't do much tonight. Got stoned and watched *The Devil's Rejects*. Gotta work in the morning. I have this constant feeling of woe. It won't go away. I'm haunted.

A muffled noise. Am I dreaming? No. It's sloppy noise.

I open my eyes and stare into the blackness. I stare in the general direction of the noise. A clatter. Something falling off my kitchen counter on to the tiled floor.

Fear spears through my heart and lungs.

My hands fumble in the darkness for the baseball bat.

I grip the *Louisville Slugger* tightly. Quietly sitting up. Slowly, tiptoeing toward the light switch.

There is someone standing in the shadows of my kitchen.

My hand rests flat against the wall and searches for the light switch.

The dark figure shuffles things around on my kitchen table.

My finger flips the light on.

We are blinded at first.

A young Native American man with thick glasses, a crewcut, and a round nose stands before me, eyes wide with fright.

I stand defiant and buck naked, hands white-knuckled around the bat.

The young man looks me up and down.

"What the fuck are you doing!?" I shout.

"Nothing," he says in an apologetic tone. "Sorry. I wanted some weed."

"Are you fucking crazy?" I scream. "Climbing in my fucking window!?"

"You didn't answer the door or your phone."

"Because I was sleeping! Take a fucking hint, you moron."

He nods. "Sorry, Natas. My sister made me do it. I'm drunk."

"I don't care! Get the fuck out of here! And don't come back! You're not fucking welcome here anymore, you fucking cocksucker!"

He nods and steps toward the door.

I cock the bat back, ready to swing. "No way, motherfucker! Leave the same fucking way you came in," I growl.

"The window?"

"Yeah, the fucking window, you fucking genius!"

He nods and climbs onto the kitchen counter and falls off onto the floor.

"Get the fuck out!" I order.

"Sorry, sorry." He climbs back up and climbs head first out the window, falling, and scrambling to his feet.

"Fucking loser!" I holler out the window after him.

I shut the window behind him and stick a 2×4 above it to hold it shut.

I smoke a cigarette to calm down and make sure he's gone, then lay back down on the couch to sleep.

As I lay there, I can't help but laugh out loud at the expression on his face when he saw me standing there naked, with bat in hand. I don't know if he was more scared of the bat or my dangling cock.

My crazy life. The other night I was sitting in a car with my brother. I had a can of mace in my hand. My poor brother was in the driver's seat with a club. When I gave him the club, he was like, "Yeh, he's a big boy, no telling what he'll do." I had no choice. I had to do business with this cat. It's a big fucking hustle and a fifty/fifty shot. He either really wanted to do business or he flipped sides and was setting me up to cause some pain. Turned out he wanted to do business. He had no idea we were prepared to take him down. I'm caught in the middle of a little war. I blame it on pop culture. *The Departed* and *The Black Donnellys*. *Scarface* and *Goodfellas*. It's madness. Think I'm a real gangsta now. Exciting as all hell, but so risky. I'm always on edge. The other day I walked into a room filled with alleged members of the Mexican Mafia. Most of them visibly carrying guns. I think of it as a social experiment. Exploration of the underworld. I have discovered a certain charismatic talent that aids me in hustling.

My wife invited me over to her house last night for sex. She's saving money for the divorce lawyer. It tears my heart up but I always come when she calls. I always cry. She always holds me and hushes me.

A band called *AM Radio Connection* writes a song about me. The third track on the EP. The song is called *Transmission Decision*. Very cool. I am very flattered. It totally rocks. It's electronica-like music. Doesn't do anything to help my growing web of madness. The singer calls me a Jedi Master. LOL. Makes me smile. I'll shut up about it now.

Freshly born, I am a child. Mad Horus.

Otto Rahn, Otto Rahn, where have you run?
Down the mountainside to sleep with Cathari?
Tangled in the Spider's web?

I call Hillary. "I just dropped off the money."
"Okay, thanks."
"Hey. I got a proposition for you. To solve our money problems."
"What's that?"
"You know a lot of people. I know a lot of people. Let's go into business together and sell pot."
"What's wrong with you, Natas?"

"Nothing. Just happy. Got myself a treat."
"What's that?"
"The new Justin Timberlake CD."
She chuckles. "What did you get me?"
"My heart."
"Oh. I want you to buy me something."
"I love you."
"Okay. Gotta go."
"What about the pot?"
"No."
"Okay."
"Bye."
"Bye."

You ever feel like the universe has got you by the balls? Like yer suddenly caught in this extreme current. Just pushing you forward, forward, forward. Everything on fast forward. Not enough time to get everything done. Can't slow down. Have to be able to make decisions on the drop of a dime. Fast quick flash. Imagining everything that could go wrong. *The Tell-Tale Heart*. There ain't a body under my floor but the moral of the story is something to live by. It becomes a mantra as the police search me. I'm well past the shaking. The greatest fear left. The po po.

I feel this natural rebellion in my heart and gut. It doesn't go away. If anything the fire burns brighter with age. My actions less definable. Initiations, transforming consciousness, willing my actions to act outside the sleepiness. Outside the cultural norms. I am beginning to understand how the process of control takes place with the energy source some call money. The evocation of it. You have to keep it rolling.

Beyond my death I'm not sure what the further goal is, besides revolution. "War is natural," my rockabilly Mexican explains as Elvis sings *Evil* from a record player in the corner of the room.

I nod. "It is Babalon. Binah. Time, creation, destruction. Kronos. Saturn. The Ouroboros cycle. The YHVH formula. The cycle continues until the godhood is realized and attained through a cleansing of the soul through a dance of lives and trials. The death anxiety created by the memory lapse of the drama is enormous and overwhelming. A sign of this new age is the technological boom of the twentieth century and the communication-information explosion. The tension between Illuminati factions is staggering. I am not saying which way these wars will go. It is a new age and a new magick. New formulas and equations. Always something new."

"What is speaking to you?" my Mexican friend asks me, lighting his pipe.

"The zeitgeist of revolution. Revolt against man and revolt against self. Revolt against any government that uses fear and violence to keep the people in line. The police are only necessary when you live in a culture with haves and have-nots.

"I do not know what I'm talking about. Ignore me."

My Mexican laughs. A pistol is on the table. "Yes you do, my friend."

"It's words, thoughts, ideas, feelings, emotions forced out of me because if it doesn't all come out I'll explode. My hand is forced by the jest of destiny."

Last night Luba asked me, "Are you still going to kill yourself?"

I was a little shocked and responded, "What do you mean? Of course not. Why do you ask me that?"

She's cuddled up next to me. "It's just that a lot of poets and artists like you always seem to kill themselves."

"Like me?"

She answered from the darkness. "Mad like you. You still don't seem very happy."

The previous night my wife and I had slept in her bed together.

The next night I kissed the blonde, blue-eyed hellion Savannah, and said, "I still want you."

Butterflies raging in my stomach. A hurricane of emotion. I feel the psychic energy seep out of me.

I am a warrior. Ronin of the Teutons and the Sioux. The evolution of revolution. I lead a one man revolution against tyranny in any way, shape or form. Stand behind me only if you have the strength to stand up and act. Only if you have the strength to awaken. Only if you have the strength to carry a soldier's weight on your shoulders. Only if you have the courage to face all fear and be consumed by destiny/free will.

I am an absolute social deviant. I am a slut. I am a criminal. I am a prophet. I do not believe my deviant behavior to be wrong. Sin is restriction. None of the behavior

I am speaking of here has caused harm to another. Most of the exhibited behavior is due to existential crisis. This point may be called the mid-life crisis. A complete shattering of the life. Reconstructed, slowly and painfully, revaluation.

Maybe I have hurt some people. Regrettably.

Magick works.

Realizing the god in control of my situation is a frightening affair and requires a tactical revision. Some of my illegal behaviors were done out of love. Some of them out of fear. Some out of the past.

A lady named Luba. Stealing kisses in the night. I'm dying in her eyes.

Nothing is certain. No thing is certain.

Speaking with ghosts on the phone. Inspiring self doubt.

Muses in the air I breath. There is only one Alexander. Only one Achilles. One Imhotep. If you know what you are, will to power. Be fearless. We are lions among men. Guided by the light of a silver star and a black sun.

Our love is like water, air, earth and fire. Our love is like no other. Walk on over, up against me. In the morning I'll be right by your side. My sweet Lux Ferro. My Luba. My sweet angel. I see dawn coming, my muse.

The chymical wedding of Lucifer and Babalon. Gravity, mathematics and sound waves come crashing down like the perfect wave rippling out from the center of the multi-verse. She lays back, smiles, and says, "It's just pussy."

If we ride this Mobius strip long enough we'll reach the end. The blind man says I can't see anything right.

Thoughts shape the universe. All of them. The universes and the thoughts.

The young god, Horus, rises to his feet.

Galabram roars, "Lions!"

Angels line the halls of heaven and hell. Armed and ready for battle. They drop like paratroopers from the sky.

I woke up at a strange house puking this morning. By chance *Andrew WK's* 'Party 'til you Puke' is playing on the stereo. Go, go, go, go, go… He's pretty right on. *Andrew WK*.

Now into the dreaming. I sit on the couch in my living room. A circle of cheap chairs left out from the night before. A TV on the floor. Framed sketches hang on the walls.

Four men in all black, top hats, and long coats surround me.

A light shines in the window.

My vision and thoughts fade to black.

Awakening aboard a star ship. The four men poke and prod at me. They are emotionless. Black eyes. Pale skin. Tall and lanky. Long, knotted fingers dangle from the black coat sleeves. They have no ears. Nostrils without noses.

Their electric voices speak to me without moving their lips. They speak like doctors or scientists.

Back in my living room a gold woman who isn't there peeks around the corner at me from the kitchen. Her body presses against mine. Pale eyes. Delicate features.

"I can't believe this," I whisper in my mind.

"Me either," she whispers in her mind.

"I love you so much."

She's naked, my hands on her buttocks. "I know you do."

I want the moment to last forever.

The black clad aliens speak in my mind with calm voices as they insert medical instruments into my flesh.

"What should I do?"

"Just relax."

Earlier that night. "I don't want her to think I like her."

"Do you like her?" Savannah squeals with excitement.

I pause. Not sure what to say. "No."

"Oh."

"What are you going to do?"

"I'm going to the bar with a Jackie. Wanna come?"

"Nah, I got some stuff to do. Need some 'me' time."

"Okay. Later."

"Later."

The aliens dress me and lead me and give me a tour of their space ship.

"That's our planet," an electric voice hums and a long finger points to a star beyond a suddenly transparent wall.

"Oh," I nod and look at the inconspicuous star among infinity.

"We are all of one."

"Oh."

"Your people do not remember where they come from. This causes the people much anxiety."

I notice a knight in a white robe with a large red cross splitting the chest into quarters and a worn out sword strapped to his hip, strolling up the hallway toward us. I ask, "So you guys can travel through space and time?"

"All dimensions."

"You see time differently than me?"

"Yes."

"Have other extraterrestrials besides you visited Earth?"

"Many live there."

"You been there since Atlantis?"

"Yes."

"Every time I see Hillary, I feel heartbroken and want to get drunk. Fucked up."

"Yes, we know."

"Can you help me with this? I mean, not get back together with her. Just get over the heartache and move on."

"The lord of the world lives in the Earth."

I just look at his egg-shaped head and black, beady eyes.

The black clad alien continues. "In 1945 we had to become more or less directly involved."

"What happened then?"

"Little Boy."

"Really. I'm not following this conversation. I don't think. And I just saw a Nazi walk by after that knight with some of your buddies. Are you guys fucking Nazis?"

Opening my eyes, I am back on my orange and brown couch.

I blink and look around the room. "Typical."

Gnosis. Is this a dream? Is this reality? Am I here? I just need. The ocean whispers in my ear. You stand and feel the current rush through your body. Rush through your body in slow motion. The light in extension. Double serpents wrapped tightly around the spine. Heads uniting as the third eye. The drums beat like tribal ghosts. Ihanktawan Dakota Teutonen. The blood of the saints drips into her holy cup. Evo, Babalon. I feel like god in you. Dance mad shaman, dance, invoke, inflame, evoke. Live, live, live and laugh. Leaping laughter. Hands and arms swim like the oracle. Soon I will return to the place of my birth. I bring a swift sword.

Saturn! Binah! Babalon! The mother of abominations! Engine of destruction! The worm of time. The sacred and scarlet whore of the temple. Goddess of time, sex and death. There can not be one without the other. She brings love and she takes it away. She brings life and she takes it away. And she give it again. The engine of creation!

Lucifer! Prometheus! My father of light and fire! My handsome prince and king archangel. Fallen renegade. My blue knight. Lover of Babalon. The emerald crown. Lord of this world, in the hollow earth, throned of Shamballah and Agarti. Gateways to heavens and hells in Mohave, Sri Lanka, the Himalayas, Antarctica. Father of the wandering ghosts of Atlantis and Lemuria. Thule and Hyperborea. Take me home to the golden age. That distorted, rose-colored memory. Illusions of a greater day. Hoka hey! We fight for a greater day!

With much bravado and spirit, the warrior shaman, the warrior monk, the ubermenschen, medicine man in vision. Bad, mad prophet of bizarre love.

There was a time, maybe, when I was a good person, I think. I don't know anymore. Can't remember. Ha. I sacrifice myself for you? I sacrifice myself for myself. There were good intentions. Always good intentions.

I am the sun. The pharaoh god. The Caesar. Let us be rogue Illuminati. Take your life in your hand and will to power.

I like the simple things in life. Solitude and friendship. Cool wet water on my lips.

A violinist with a triangular head plays and even plucks. He sits on my shoulder like nightmare.

I am low. Low to the earth. Lower than you think. I bow and kneel, lay flat beneath you. Kiss your feet.

Belief system is the cat in the box.

Oh, my. 11:11 is 47 and 74. 4+7=11. 47:74. There is a synchronistic loop here. Between the years 1947 and 1974. Many strange important esoteric occurrences. The opening of the 11:11 gateway. It began with things such as my spiritual Jack Parsons' and the trickster L. Ron Hubbard's work. They were Dee and Kelley. Correlating to the death of uncle Crowley, the possession of the Lizard King, the UFO explosion into popular consciousness, etc. In 1974 the oddities were things such as Phillip K. Dick's *Valis* and the impeachment/sacrifice of Nixon and Robert Anton Wilson's contact with his Holy Guardian Angel and Timothy Leary's telepathy experiments.

It is a gateway. The 11:11. The pillars of Solomon. The pillars of Heracles. The pillars of the Tree of Life. Ascension is between the pillars. The path of the righteous. Occasional sightings of 11:11 suggest peak moments. Guideposts. The scarab is knocking at the window. The initiation process balanced up the Middle Pillar like a bullet aimed at God's heart. This entrance. Ride the snake. 11 × 11 builds the pyramids. 23 chromosomes plus 23 chromosomes plus spirit equals 47. Daath is 11. We be Baldur and Tammuz. This is Galahad and Perseus. Jachim and Boaz.

The Galabram mythos.

———◆———

I love music. I love art. I love words. Logos, you dig? It all moves me.

I look around the living room at my group of oddballs and eccentrics. They sit in a circle on the wood floor. An old, unpolished, and worn hardwood floor. Long-haired Erik explaining to everyone that the United States is not really a democracy. The hyper Byron, wearing an *In Fames* t-shirt. Joss, naive with a flair for drama and the gift of gab. An old Vietnam vet named Texas who is always dressed like a rhinestone cowboy and buys weed from me every week with his disability check. The intelligent and lippy Jim. A silverback gorilla-sized Native American named Marv Two Eagles is passed out on the floor. A hyperactive weight lifter/waiter is doing an animated and outrageous Chris Farley impersonation. His name is Shad. He buys dope from me, too. A young, pretty girl with thick brown eyebrows, going on and on about her recently completed political science degree.

There is Max, an African-American Christian musician/undercover cop in the kitchen, arm wrestling with my friend Hoss, a mad, muscle-bound Asgardian brick layer. There are about 40 people in the one bedroom apartment. The music is loud. Right now sublime is singing 'Caress Me Down' from vibrating black pillars. The electronic altar blinks and flashes like a hypnotic drone. We are wild. Feral.

The back door is wide open. People wander in and out smoking cigarettes and joints, bottles wag in their fevered hands.

On the coffee table surrounded by a procession of diverse beer cans, wine bottles, ash trays, burning candles, and incense. In the center of the table a two pound loose pile of green and elvish marijuana. A pile of various pills next to that. Little blue ones. White ones. Yellow ones. Pink ones with arching dolphins etched on them.

There is close to three hundred more pounds of the grass in a closet. In another room the plants themselves

Confessions of a Black Magician

growing under artificial light, and still another dark and humid room with rows of large shelves of glass canning jars growing the mushrooms.

The digital clock on the wall blinks "3:49 a.m." I hear laughter. Someone shouts, "I fart perfume and shit rose petals!"

Another guy I don't really know stands in the corner of the living room. He's a blue collar guy, talking to a black guy from Detroit, Jesse. I catch a snippet of their conversation. The blue collar guy says, "See! I told you! Every conversation when you're at the bar ends up coming down to either Adolph Hitler and the Nazis or defecation."

"Hey," Erik asks the circle, "do you know what I'm trying to say?"

I look at his long, flapping hair and blue headband and answer, "No."

"Oh."

"Hit it once for me!" Byron grins at Luba and me.

I just look at him and smile.

My fiery Luba screams, "Fuck you, Byron!" Punches him hard on the shoulder.

He lets out an hysterical giggle.

A blond, athletic Nazi skinhead in red suspenders and tight blue jeans tucked into black leather combat boots pokes my shoulder. "Hey, I'm going to Florida to sell magazines door to door." He has swastikas tattooed on his hands. A few months from now he will go to prison in Florida for murder.

"Awesome," I nod, still holding Luba's gentle, firm hand, imagining I can feel her heart beating in her fingertips. Why oh why oh why oh why oh. I think about the three thousand dollars bulging in my faded leather wallet…and the rest under the floorboard.

She whispers in my ear, "You're so cool." Her lips tickle. Her breath soft.

I look around the room and what I can see of the kitchen, spotting my enforcers. My soldiers. About two dozen in all. Only three here tonight. Marv passed out on the floor. Shad doing Chris Farley. Big man Clint in the kitchen arm wrestling with Hoss.

"Play some blues," Luba whispers in my ear, licking it.

I step over to the electronic altar and my fingers glide across the keyboard. Old, wise *Son House* claps his hands from within the black vibrating pillars and sings out in a gravely voice, *"Who's that riding? John the Revelator..."*

Byron's head bobs with a cool smile.

"Keep that door shut now," pointing at the kitchen door and talking to Byron. I turn the music down.

Luba pulls on my hand toward the bedroom. I follow.

Jim changes the music when the bedroom door shuts. 'Pimps' by *The Coup* starts playing.

It ain't over.

She always takes the godform of Lucifera.

Luba has us falling on the bed as fast as I shut the door. Her body is hard and firm. Full lips. Small breasts. Cute dimples over her ass cheeks. She talks nasty. Sometimes I just blush.

Serenity is passed out in the bed next to our panting bodies.

On the bed across from us a naked couple is passed out, bodies tangled, breathing loud. The guy is snoring.

Serenity wakes up, smiling at us. A warm smile. She kisses Luba on the mouth and opens her legs, pressing my hand between her thighs.

I think of sigils. Picture them in my mind as Dax Riggs sings from the living room stereo. *"Dressed up in smoke and yellow wolf's skin...we spin and spin..."*

The walls breathe and sweat and bleed in some places. The shadows move and dance with secret life. Morphing skeletons creep and tease from the darkest spots. I realize they're other people in here, aren't there? I sense them. People that aren't there. Spirit beings standing around watching us. The ghosts of my mother and father. Al and H.P. Others, too. Some on the ceiling. One kneeling at the bed, examining our holy trinity.

My entire body spasms in pure ecstasy at the pressure of both women's bodies. They moan and click. Their bodies and souls swirl with mine.

I rest on my back between the two. Their legs draped over me. A delicate hand on my breathing chest. A head resting safely on my shoulder. I stare at the ceiling and listen to the music coming from the other room mixed with a murmur of voices. I watch the shadows as they slow. My mouth dry. Cold sweat. Staring at the flat ceiling. The plaster walls. I've been drinking beer tonight. *Pabst Blue Ribbon* and *New Castle*. I've been smoking pot. I've been doing lines of coke. I ate some acid a few hours ago.

I am a devil and I'm going straight to hell. My mind raging in eternity. Haunted and flailing.

The music stops playing. Morning birds chirp outside. The sun rises in the east, shining through the blinds.

I zombie walk into the living room, leaving Luba and Serenity in their sweet slumber. Byron and his blond afro friend are sitting on the couch. On the loveseat, some black-haired kid in a *Misfits* t-shirt I don't recognize.

"Hey," the red eyed Byron grins at me.

The other kid vigorously puffs on a cigarette butt.

"That's Billy," Byron slurs.

I nod and try not to step on the mounds of sleeping bodies scattered throughout the living room as I make my way toward the kitchen.

A knock at the door.

Panic.

Byron and Billy the Kid come into the kitchen with me, hands over their mouths, whispering to me, "Who is it?" Frantically looking around the kitchen for an escape.

I shrug with a still hand on the doorknob.

Looking at the clock, where did the time go?

"Who is it?" My voice dry.

"Your neighbor," a male voice answers through the wood door.

I open the door just a crack and peek my eye out, seeing my big, gruff hipster neighbor, Marlin. I open the door the rest of the way.

"Hey, Natas, I'll give you twenty bucks for gas if you take me to get my new furniture with your truck, man."

"Um." I look back at the people lying on the floor and step outside, closing the door behind me. "Okay. Let's go."

"Oh," he makes a victorious fist. "Very cool, man," and gives a genuine smile behind his shades.

We walk to my truck. The sun seems so bright. The air is crisp. I stand and look at my old truck, thinking this is weird. Wait. I'm way too fucked up to drive. I'm still tripping balls. Okay. Stop. But I am not drunk anymore. Or am I? I can't tell. I am definitely not high off weed anymore.

My neighbor reaches for the truck's silver door handle. He's a hip construction worker. His sleeves are cut off showing off colorful tattoos.

"Um…hey," I muse.

"Yeah?" Pausing, he raises his eyebrows high with a big grin. "What's up?"

"I can't drive. I'm too fucked up."

"Fucked up?" He smiles and frowns. "On what?"

"I'm tripping on acid."

"Whoa, dude." He laughs, raising and waving his hands. "Get back inside. I'll figure something else out, man, no problem."

I shrug and hold out my keys. "You can use it if you want."

"You sure?"

"Yeah." I think, *"he's a hipster, he's harmless."*

I walk over to the mail box and check the mail. Feeling utterly confused. I don't know why I'm checking the mail. I had taken the truck key off my key ring when I gave it to Marlin.

Looking at the neighbor sitting in my truck, a sexy, dark-haired hipster bird smiles and waves at me before she climbs into the passenger's seat.

Who is she? Don't know. Never saw her before. Wait. Maybe I have seen her at a hipster bar? I don't know. Don't care. Fucking hipsters.

Back inside my apartment. The mountain range of sleeping bodies still cover the floor.

"What's going on?" Byron stands in the kitchen smoking a cigar and drinking from a plastic jug of orange juice.

"The neighbor. He wanted me to move stuff. No. He wanted me to drive him. Or he wanted to use my truck. Fuck. I can't explain. That was way too fucking weird to deal with."

Byron laughs and sits down on the couch watching a movie on the television.

Billy the Kid is back on the loveseat.

I can hear them all breathing, their hearts beating, dreaming.

Another knock on the door. I'm still in the kitchen. This one louder and faster. Urgent.

I open the door. Clint is standing there with a big, dopey grin and his thick arms full of two wine crates under stacks of frozen steaks. "I went to the hotel."

"I thought you went home."

"No." He sets his goods on the kitchen counter, giving me a chuckle, "I got more shit out in the car. Come on. Help me carry it in."

Billy the Kid and Byron go outside and help Clint haul everything in. Sometimes I think I should call him "ox". He is tall with thick limbs. Just a burly motherfucker. A crazy Hitler-style haircut. Except his hair is blond. He even has the moustache. I don't get his style, but whatever.

I stand in the kitchen watching them haul everything in. More wine and frozen steaks. Champagne. Whiskey. Cartons of cigarette. Fresh fruit. Byron munches on a banana. Erik wakes up and joins in the summer morning festivities.

Clint bellows, "Wulf wants to know if you still want to hit the safe at that taco place?"

I look at Billy the Kid in the living room watching TV and look back at Clint. "Would you shut up. Fucking hell."

"What?" He gives me an exaggerated shrug peppered with a look of innocence. "Fuck him. I'll slap the shit out of him right now. He won't say a fucking word."

"No," I shake my head, "leave him alone. Just watch your mouth, alright? I'm leaving for a while. I just gotta go. I'll be back later."

"Okay," he shrugs, opening a package of steak and placing a frying pan on the stove. "Where you going?"

"I'm going to go outside and smoke this cigarette and then I'm gonna go buy some more."

"Okay. I'll be here," he grins.

"Yeah, hold down the fort with Byron and Erik. Don't let anyone else in."

"Gotcha."

I walk back outside into the sunlight, feeling like the undead. Following the cracked side walk. Blocks and blocks. Crossing streets. Watching cars drive by. Cops freak me out. It's early summer. I walk up to a familiar/unfamiliar house. Knock on the door. Hillary answers with a scowl etched into her face.

"What do you want?" she hisses at me with venom on her claws.

I look at the shag carpet beneath her small, bare feet. Little toes. "I just need a place to sleep."

"Sleep at your house," barking, her hand on her hip, elbow at a right angle. A tight wife-beater and no bra. I can see the color of her nipples through the shirt. Arousing me even though I feel like crying.

"I can't stay at my house."

She sighs, pushes her glasses onto her forehead. "Why not? I can't wait to fucking hear this. You're a fucking disaster."

"I just need a safe place to sleep for awhile."

She sighs again. "Okay. Come in. Keep your hands to yourself. I'm cleaning. You can sleep in the bedroom."

"Thank you," I mumble and make my way to the bedroom. She doesn't love me anymore. I take off my red shoes. Strip to my boxers and get between clean sheets and a warm, fluffy comforter. Smells nice. Relax. Soft asylum. Drifting quickly to sleep. Like a babe in the arms of a mother.

That night everything feels beautiful. Wind blows through my chest. Every note immaculate. I love the fucking music! Tonight everything is perfect. Um. I think I might disappear for a while. Not sure when that's gonna happen, but the snowball is big enough that I know it is going to happen. Ha. And I love Luba. And Luba loves me for now. Just in time to watch it all shatter, she stands ready to walk away from all the pieces. She is everything cool.

Late morning. I keep on driving.

I drive out to the temple of Pan again. In the center of a small forest off a dusty country road.

Avoiding everyone's phone calls. Got the ringer on silent.

Maybe I joined so many cults and magickal orders that things got fucked up. They got twisted somehow. The currents intermingled. Like in *Ghostbusters*. Don't cross the streams. Not completely sure what's real anymore. Imagination? Reality? Astral? Akashic?

After sitting all day and watching the sun lower in the sky, I walk back to the truck. The sun shining through the trees and leaves across my vision as I stroll reminds me of a dream machine. When I get to the truck the sun is red.

I was the fool. The hermit. The hierophant. The magus. The lovers. The devil. The knight of swords. Lust. Justice. The chariot. The kings and queens of all ages.

I go home and do the etheric boogie. Visit a hawk-headed god. A voyeuristic Apollo stands with the flirting Eros and Cupid.

I tell them, "I want to be king of Antarctica."

When the ritual is over I take off walking down the night street for some fresh air.

I am Sol. Helios. Osiris. I am centered in Tiphareth. Others of my path be John and Simon.

And the black magician just keeps on riding, baby. It's just the way it is. It is what it is, man. Life keeps rolling. With or without you.

You don't get off your ass and roll with it, it'll roll right over you.

Through it all I kept writing. Never stop writing. At the expense of it all, write on.

Tonight I look into her pale blue eyes. She's immaculate. Possibilities flutter around my mind. Parallel universes. That's all there are. The classic moments. The initiations. Tiny deaths.

Ah, this super cool clown. This fool.

I feel the sun on my face through the window. It's dead outside. The passage through the underworld.

Sojourn to *Kublai Khan*.

I'm somewhere in this dream.

———⟫✦⟪———

I shut off communications with the, hmm, the current. The omens. The secret chiefs. They stand in wait. My life is not my own. Choose to be chosen. We are lions and make no pacts with men. 13 strong in this city and riding the Galabram current.

I sing for joy. Bring me Monday. Bring me Lucifer. Bring life and light and holy fire. Bring love and joy and limitless freedom.

Given up all hope. I sacrificed myself. The canary in the cage. Poured myself into hell. Shaped in inferno. Crowley knew only the strong survive.

I am god. This is not unique.

I've seen the full moon shimmer and twirl and quake and beat like a heart. Grow and breathe in a glorious illuminating.

Huh? Whatever, man…

"Natas, my nigga, I thought you were coming over right away." Jim is sitting on my couch smoking a blunt. Legs up on the coffee table, an arm around Nada.

"Um. I was. I got sidetracked, distracted. I'm a leaf blowing in Zen wind. I'm Casanova giving out blood roses to all the women I've loved before. I'm so low down, down low, way down, so far down. You shine like a beacon in the night, in my dreams, you haunt my heart like a ghost in my soul. We're star-crossed diamonds counting hallelujahs in the rain.

"We are lions, gold and roaring, the pride of the underground. You're so bold and noble, king and queen, only god knows if I'm holding all aces and spades and who's got the joker and wild card. To be alive the worlds must collide. So return to the temple of Pan on moon day or Saint John's summer day. IAO Pan! IAO Pan! The temple is elemental and we are sublime.

"I'm out of cigarettes and about to shave my head. And I ask myself, "What should I do? What should I do?" About her and her and her. And the substance D.

"Lay me down in the street. Still have hints of a plan coming together, oh, so slow. What do I have left to work with? Artist, writer, magician. It's a start, but what do I want to do with my life now? Hmm. I don't know. I'm searching. Existentially necessary for me to re-establish a footing and climb Maslow's pyramid again. I pursue purpose."

"Fuck," Jim chuckles, handing me the blunt. "Sometimes I don't know what the hell you're talking about, you god damned cutter!"

The alarm shocks me from sleep.

I fumble from the couch to the end table, slapping the snooze button on top of the alarm clock. The room is silent again. I roll over, curling up under the blanket. My pillow is wet with drool. Back to red dreams of Babalon. I am Lucifer blue.

The alarm goes off. I struggle to open my eyes and focus on the clock. Snooze goes off nine minutes after the button is hit. I better get up. I have shit to do today. My hand surrenders and shuts the alarm off instead of another snooze.

I inspect the coffee table. Everything is in order. I gulp water from a bottle and swish it around in my mouth. The remote clicks the television on with the volume muted. Another remote turns the stereo on. Drums beat. 'Sex and Violence' by *The Exploited*. I pick a glass pipe up off the

table, sit up, hit it a few times. Followed by the usual cigarette. I sit and listen to the music.
   I look at my phone. Forty-two missed calls. Thirteen texts. How fast can you move? Oh, I yawn and stretch. Top of the morning to you. I brush my teeth in the shower, singing along to 'Sex and Violence'. The song is on repeat.
   After the shower I stand naked looking through my clothes. Jot notes in my magickal diary. A few more hits. Another cigarette. Turn the music up. Dance a bit. The phone rings. It's Gianna. She wants pot. Wants to know if I want to go to a party tonight.
   Maybe.
   I get dressed.
   Uh. Four deliveries to make today. Six collects. Gotta meet some people for some disk golf this afternoon.
   I hustle out the door and to my truck. Shad and his girlfriend are outside. She says, "Geez, Natas, you always dress like a rock star."
   I blush and get in the truck.
   I drive out into the country. My favorite thing to do. Drive around in the country smoking joints. Burn cruise. That usually takes up at least an hour of my day. I write poetry as I drive around listening to loud music. Jim's all into the underground hip hop scene, but he's been asking me about punk rock lately. Like he doesn't get it, but he wants to because he's got punk rock friends. Which is cool.
   Luba is in jail. I've been all somber about that. But I'm still having fun.
   Okay, I make my stops. Everything runs smoothly and my wallet is full of cash by the time I disk. Which takes another hour. I have more errands to run.
   I feel like I've done everything. Like I'm exhausted and bored. Nothing's shocking. None of it means anything

anymore. I'm just an actor on stage. Things seem to be going so fast. I can't keep up. Dizzy. More like I'm watching a movie than living my own life. So many people. I don't even like a lot of them.

I'll build my empire like this.
You will not understand this.
It starts raining out. A heavy rain.
The angel on my left is Lucifer blue. The angel on my right Babalon red.

The angel Galabram and the prophet Abraham materialize in the seat next to me as I drive into the country for my second burn cruise. They've become overprotective brethren. Arguing. I try not to listen to their riddles.

Sick of my iPod, I turn on the radio. "Hate Me" by *Blue October* starts.

Tears well up in my eyes.

Galabram and Abraham stop arguing and just sit quietly looking out the window at the fields passing by.

I bite my lip and tears stream down my cheeks.

Why am I always fucking up?

I thought Luba was going to save me and now she's gone, too.

I thought they were all going to save me.

"It'll be okay," Abraham says in a grandfatherly voice.

The Atlantean Galabram nods in agreement.

The DJ announces the premiere of this new song, the album hasn't even been released yet.

Okay.

The song starts. *Rihanna* 'Umbrella'.

I start smiling and laughing, singing with the song. Bouncing in my seat.

As I drive back into town I jot down another short poem.

My red cell phone rings. I don't recognize the number. "Hello?"

"Hi! Is this Natas?" a perky young female voice asks.

"Who is this?"

"You don't know me."

"How'd you get my number?"

"Luba gave it to me in jail. Hey. Everybody knows you."

"Really."

"We've met before."

"Where?"

"At a party by your house. A few weeks ago. I was there with my brother."

"I don't remember."

"We sat outside on the curb."

"You're lying."

"You just don't remember."

"What are you calling for?"

"I wanna hang out. Party with you."

"No, this is too weird." I feel dried tears on my cheeks as I speak.

"What's weird?"

"Some weird bird calling me out of the blue and wanting to hang out."

"Oh, come on. I know all about you."

"Are you a cop? Working for the cops?"

She giggles. "No."

"How do I know that? How do I know you're not wearing a wire right now?"

"Come pick me up right now and you can strip search me."

"Alright. Where you at?"

"Pick me up on the corner of 18th Street and Center Avenue."

"Okay. What's yer name?"

"Layla."

After hanging up the phone, I hit my joint one last time and throw it out the window as I drive to pick up this new mystery bird.

By the time I get there the late afternoon rain is gone from the sky and it's hot and humid. Sticky hot again.

I'm stunned as I pull up to the corner where she's waiting for me. She's really cute. Giving me the most beautiful pearly smile. Purple and black sunglasses. Long brown hair. Slender with large breasts. Short shorts. A tight baby blue shirt showing off her midriff. White and pink sparkly letters on her chest read "pimp". An inny belly button. She reminds me of some Anime chick come to life or something.

"Hi," she waves and she hops in. Freckles sprinkle across her cheeks and nose. Big green eyes. She's half white and half Asian.

"Hey," I say from behind sunglasses.

She smiles, ever smiling, just bubbly and bright, cheerful. "Let's go somewhere and get high where you can search me for the wire."

"Okay." I nod and turn up the music. *Bronze Nazareth* 'The Pain'.

The city is alive. I watch the people wander through my little city.

A young man in jogging pants and no shirt with a gold necklace jumps up onto a block wall next to the sidewalk. He runs along the wall, hopping off with a triumphant grin as his feet hit the pavement.

Layla talks and talks. I just listen to the music. I don't know the people she's talking about. Man, she is fine looking. Her boobs are huge. On such a tiny body.

"Where you wanna go?" I ask, trying to watch the road.

She gives me doe eyes with a pout. "Your house."

"Why?"

"Let's get some beer, get stoned, and have a party at your house."

"You're fucking crazy. You don't know me."

"I know who you are. You're a gangster. A drug dealer."

"What're you talking about?" I laugh and shake my head.

"I know." She leans close, lowering her voice. "I've heard about all the crazy stuff you do."

I wonder about a sigil.

"Come on," she whines.

"Why should I trust you? I don't know you."

She pulls her shirt up.

I keep glancing between the street and her firm breasts as I drive.

She pulls her shirt back down, giggling. "No wire." She shimmies her shorts down to her thighs. "See."

"Alright, man. We'll see what we can stir up."

"Yippee!" She claps her hands and bounces in her seat.

Later that evening Layla, Jim, Mike and myself sit around the living room, drinking beer, smoking pot, listening to music, and talking. The sun is still up and all the windows are open. The curtains blow.

Mike's girlfriend shows up and he leaves with her. A few minutes later Gianna and a girlfriend of her's come to the door. We drive to the gas station to get more beer. I joke with Gianna about wearing a wire, too. She gleefully shows us her boobs and no wire. Gianna is a bitch, but she makes money for me. I don't trust her. She flaunts a romantic interest in me when it's obvious she's only interested in business and bank.

When we get back, Jim and Layla are sitting in the living room, laughing and talking with Briana. She's there to buy weed. Jim and I work with her. Yes, I have a new job. Working as little as possible, it's really just a front to explain where my money comes from.

I give her a sack in the kitchen and place a pound in the cupboard next to the refrigerator. She sticks the pot in her purse. We join everyone in the living room.

Gianna and Jim are playfully arguing about hip hop. Jim kicks his shoes off. Gianna says she likes *TI*.

I look at the coffee table. It's covered in beer cans. Various pills lay scattered between empty beer cans. An empty baggy. Overflowing ash tray.

"This is a cool place you have here," Briana compliments.

"It's not his place," Jim tattles.

Briana scrunches her face and shrugs.

"It's a friend's place," I reply.

"Why are we here?" Layla asks.

I shrug and take swig of beer. "I'm just laying low. Don't want a lot of traffic at my place anymore."

"Detectives keep stopping by Natas' crib." Jim nods. "Joss had to go on the run. He spilt to California. Who knows?"

I know Briana likes metal, so being a good host I ask her if she wants to hear *Acid Bath* rather than this underground hip hop. I apologize because *Acid Bath* is the only metal I have at this house.

She wants to hear it.

I'm feeling pretty buzzed up. Pretty carefree and happy. I put on *Acid Bath*. 'The Blue' screeches to life and turns into low, slow, heavy beating. The singer roars.

"Come on," Jim moans melodramatically, "turn this cutter shit off."

"Ha," I point at him. "No. Just listen. It's really fucking good."

He reaches for the CD player.

I grab his hand. "No way. I'll fight you for it."

"Ha, ha, ha," Jim laughs. "You can't stop me, old man."

I laugh and tackle him. We wrestle to the ground. It lasts for several minutes. We both give up when the girls yell at us to knock it off. We join them back in the living room, both winded. Achilles and a Spartan.

"Shit," Jim says, "gimme that joint." He snatches it from Briana.

She looks shocked and laughs. "You guys do this all the time?"

"Pretty much." Jim nods like an aristocrat.

"Hey," Giana gives a cheerful yell at Jim. "Don't blow that marijuana smoke in my face. I have to take a piss test."

Jim laughs and blows again.

"You fucker." She punches him on the arm.

Everyone is laughing. 'Bones of Baby Dolls' is playing on the stereo.

A loud knock at the door makes everyone jump.

I go to the door and look through the peep hole. I can see three police officers. The one in front knocking is an

Asian with braces on his teeth. Maybe more behind these three. I can't tell. I turn and look back at everyone, panic stricken, I whisper, "The pigs."

Jim gets up and runs to the back of the house.

"You have to open your door, sir."

"No, I don't."

"We're here because of a noise complaint."

"Sorry, I'll turn the music down."

"You have to open the door, sir."

"Why?"

"Because I have to see your face."

"Why do you have to see my face?"

"To make sure everything is okay."

"Everything is fine." I look back at the others. Briana is gone somewhere. Gianna, her friend, and Layla sit frozen on the couch. "I'm turning the music off and going to bed."

"I'll be forced to open this door if you don't, sir."

"Really?"

"I have to see your face."

"Okay, just a peek."

Gently, I unlock the door. A feeling of disembodiment comes over me. I open the door, just a crack, and put my foot in front of it. As I peek, the Asian cop slams his body against the door, forcing it open. My foot doesn't work as a door stopper and my ankle is nearly broken before I can get out of the way. I stagger backwards as four armed police officers enter the house. Two of them search the house. The other two question me. The Asian with the braces does all the talking, the other one just gives me a cold stare.

They ask me my name and a series of routine questions, leading up to, "So where's the marijuana?"

"The what?" I say.

"We heard the girl talking about it. We smell it."

"Oh. Maybe it's cigarettes."

"Layla isn't old enough old enough to be drinking."

"Oh. I didn't know." I'm getting confused.

"We weren't drinking," Gianna barks.

A cop comes back from the other side of the house holding Briana by the arm. "Why were you hiding?"

"Who's this?" One of my cops asks me. "I thought you said there wasn't anyone else here."

"What's this," the fourth cop holds a beer can with an extinguished roach atop it and an empty baggy in his other hand.

"Yes, what is that?" the Asian asks me while his partner begins snooping around, opening cupboards. My heart races.

Fuck it, I think to myself, it's over. I'm done in. It's fucking over. "I don't know."

The Asian grins at me, showing off his silver braces. "Well, guess what, Natas. You're under arrest for the possession of marijuana."

I nod. Calm. Resigned.

"Let me see your identification, ma'am," a cop says to Briana.

She picks up her purse to get her driver's license out.

The cop takes the purse away and rifles through it. Eureka, he holds up a clear baggy of marijuana. "Is this yours?" He looks at Briana.

She looks like a deer caught in headlights, forcing herself to nod.

Oh. The Asian cop is putting my hands behind my back. He's my new friend. Handcuffs. Cold, uncomfortable, hard metal. I am bound. My hands behind my back.

The Asian cop asks me, "Whose shoes are those?"

"Mine."

"You're wearing yours."

"Here he is," a cop shouts from the back of the house. A moment later he comes walking out with his hand on Jim's shoulder. "He was hiding under the bed. Why do you suppose he was doing that?" He chuckles.

My cop leads me out the door and the voices inside fade. It's night outside. But still warm enough for shorts and t-shirt. As I try to count the steps, I know it will only be a matter of time until they find what I stuck in the cupboard and the drugs on the coffee table. Two felonies? Maybe more. Plus the pot charge. With the recent record I got, I'm fucked.

The silver-toothed Asian sits me in the back of his car. I see Briana in handcuffs being led out to another patrol car.

Oh, I've lost the sun.

The cop stands there with the door open. Leaning down. One arm on the roof of the car, the other on the top of the door. He's young. Younger than me. Nice looking guy if he didn't have the braces on his teeth and that fucking cop haircut. You know. He looks friendly. If he weren't a cop I'd sell dope to him. "So, you going to tell me where you got the pot, Natas? Make things easier on yourself?"

The radio in his car and on his belt hiss with static. He switches the one on his belt off.

I look up at him from with my hands bound behind my back, a sincere expression, and ask, "Is there no help for a widow's son?"

"Excuse me." He looks baffled.

"I plead the fifth amendment, sir."

"Oh, you do, do you? Fine. Have it your way." With a touch of anger in his voice, he slams the car door shut hard. Not giving me time to get out of the way. It hits my side. I grunt and move out of the way before he slams it against me again.

He struts around to the driver's side and gets in the car.

"What am I being arrested for?"

"Possession of marijuana."

He starts to drive.

"How much do you think it will cost to get out?"

"Maybe a hundred bucks if you call a bail bondsman."

"You mind turning some music on?"

"Shut the fuck up."

I shrug, nod and wait.

Two hours later I'm walking from the police station to the house we were arrested at.

I call Jim on my cell as I walk.

He picks me up with his car.

We discuss the night's events.

Jim shakes his head. "They took everybody."

"Everybody?"

"Yeah."

"Oh, God, that's so horrible. What the fuck's going to happen now?"

"They gave me a ticket. I have to go to court. I'll probably go to jail."

"How long do you think?"

"A week maybe."

"That sucks. Fuck, the night started off so great. I'm broke now, too."

We get back to the house. I check and they didn't find anything. I pack it all up. Time to move. Jim and I each have a beer.

"Jesus fucking H. Christ on a crutch, how the fuck did they not find all this pot. And the pills all over the table. I thought I was going to prison! Holy shit. I gotta clean this place up."

"I'll come over after work today and help clean," Jim offers.

I look at the time. It's five in the morning. I have to work in three hours.

At work that morning the boss yells at me for being out of it. I just want to cry.

The next day our arrests are in the newspaper and on the local news stations.

A black brother does not choose to be a black brother on the surface. The magician makes an error in judgment at some point during initiation and becomes a black brother while continuing to believe he or she is still a white, yellow or black magician. This most often occurs during the crossing of the abyss.

The first step in redemption, what we'll call it for the moment, is to admit one has become a black brother, which is not easy, for who wants to admit failure. The first step in correcting any problem is first admitting there is a problem.

After my last journal entry, a few mornings after my marijuana arrest, I come home covered in blood. Not my blood. It is the blood of three different people. People who owed me money.

Looking at myself in the mirror, covered in this blood, been drinking and smoking and snorting for about three days with no sleep. I can't explain what happened, but I've had enough.

That afternoon I go to an outpatient treatment center downtown for a chemical dependency assessment. The counselor doing the assessment just stares at me in her office with her mouth hanging open. She calls in her supervisor and two more counselors. They decide I need an emergency placement in an inpatient treatment center.

I sit there sweating, lazily gazing out the window at the street. Mindless traffic zips back and forth. A homeless Native American guy stands in front of a liquor store panhandling for change.

"Uh. Yeah. That's all fine with me. I want to go to treatment."

Nobody knows. None of my friends. My illegal Mexican. Luba. Nobody. I'm just going to disappear for a while.

Part Four

Rosa Virgo

"The magi is the paradoxal man. The man-god. He knows he will not know God and this knowledge is the link to the unknown, the hidden God, making it known. Unknown and known. The Paradoxal Man God."
— Eliphas Levi, *Paradoxes of the Highest Science*

Before my treatment begins I have to detox. It takes several days. I don't remember much of it. It's all a dreamy haze. I do remember stomach cramps. Cold sweats. My hands shaking. Puking. Dry heaves. Wanting to die until one morning in the treatment center I wake up, feeling a little better. The sun shines outside. They move me to another room to begin my therapy.

I feel I've finally reached the point where I can leave my divorce and all this horseshit behind me.

Now this is it. I'm truly alone. This is the ticket to ride. I'm in treatment. I feel very alone. There are a lot of people here, but I don't want to talk with them. Why not? They ain't hip. They don't know. I need my elite, esoteric soldiers.

I have to face drug charges when I get out of this place. There are still detectives snooping me. Causes a bit of anxiety, but I don't think I'll catch a case. I get to keep my job when I'm discharged, but can't afford to live off of that money. The job was just a front for my cash flow. I can't afford it without selling drugs and robbing anymore. I don't know what the future holds.

Treatment is so boring.

I have to find my center. Find some goodness still deep in me somewhere. Be a father and husband again. A writer and an artist. Pay off my fines.

I'm afraid of everything.

This treatment is further initiation. The beginning of a new working to guide myself out of the nomadic ravings of the abyss. I am dead. I am in the womb again.

The journals are necessary for the work.

The bastard clan fights to live.

It's family day. No family here to see me. No friends here to visit. I've finished the initial paperwork they give to all treatment center clients, and now I'm alone in a quiet, little chapel. Wish I could sleep in here. There is a comforting silence in this chapel, even with the murmur of voices outside the door.

I'm afraid of so many things. I need to feel God. What does it wants from me? No prison, please. Freedom and love, please. I want to be a good man again. I want to be an instrument of God.

I need to find a *King James Bible*. All I seem to find around here are little orange-covered copies of the *New Testament*. And tiny glimpses of what the future may bring.

My room number is 210 (TOPAN) and directly across the hall from my room is an elderly Indian alcoholic named Bellaron. Eerily close to Belarion, the antichrist name Jack Parsons had chosen. I was so naïve with the Babalon Isis Working, thinking I would pass through the Black Odyssey quickly. I understand now that one must guide oneself to the end of the pilgrimage. Admitting the mistake of becoming a black brother is my first step in the right direction.

I can't sleep. I hate being alone. I want God in my life. I need God in my life. Need to touch it, feel it, hear it, see it, be consumed by it.

It's a hot humid summer. Very hot. Very humid. I think I have 27 days left of treatment.

God, is there a future for me? I've fucked up my life so much. I had built up such a good and successful life and threw it all away with such ease and zeal. God, help me through these hard times. Let me become your servant again. I'd like to continue with the magick, but like Enoch and those who walk with God. I want to walk a righteous path but don't know how.

It doesn't matter what anyone thinks of me anymore. I was afraid to let people see me reading the bible at first. Thought they would think light of it, that I am a Christian. I no longer fear this. My God is the God of Abraham.

The other day the pastor met with me here at the treatment center. He said the devil is happy that he won me over, but we will win me back.

I return, I return, I return.

I offer myself to God, my Lord.

If God sends me to jail or prison, God has a reason for it and it will not be forever. All holy men disappear for a time and return. I have been gone for some time and now know my path to return. God will decide if I go to prison or jail. I beg and pray not.

I have nightmares almost every night. Last night the nightmare felt so real it took a moment of wakefulness to realize it was only a dream. I dreamed that something was pounding on the door, trying to get in. I stood silent and frightened before the door, refusing to open it.

Even in waking I remember and know what intangible demon pounds at my soul.

The nurses here tell me I have high blood pressure. Kidney damage. Liver damage.

I recite the prayer of St. Francis several times a day.

I want to scream because I'm such a drama queen.

The resident shrink says there is nothing wrong with me on a mental health level except that I have an eating disorder. It's the first time I've been accused of that.

Every few days I call the police station from a pay phone in the treatment center's lobby to see if there are warrants for my arrest. There never are.

Abraham came from the land of Ur. Sumer. Which Sumerian deity is the God of the *Old Testament*?

I've been chanting mantras alone in my room. Quietly. Not to make a spectacle. Sometimes I chant YHVH. My roommate is an old, homosexual alcoholic. He seems pretty rough and beat up by life. I don't mind him at all. He's a nice guy, even though his feet stink really bad and he snores really loud. I wear ear plugs for his snoring. He leaves me alone when I'm meditating in our room.

I've started running. Two miles, four times a week. I must heal myself in body, mind and spirit.

Spiritually I am moving again.

It's a long road back from hell and every step strengthens me. I don the armor of God in the psychical world.

Lion of Sion.

And carry the Sword of Abraham, Isaac and Israel.

My rockabilly illegal Mexican contacted me here in treatment. A phone call. He explained to me that they ran into an old rival of mine and as a favor tossed him in a dumpster behind the bar they were at. I thanked him for the respect and explained to him I would no longer be working with the mafia once I'm discharged from treatment.

He laughed and said he would like me to keep working with them, explaining that I earn a lot of money for them and move shit fast. I said, "Sorry, but I am changing my life." I felt fear in my gut. Would they come after me? He sighed after a moment of silence and said in a thick accent, "You play this game for now Natas. But if we ever see or hear of you hustling again, we'll come back to you. Understand?"

"Yes," I replied. I understood this meant I was not allowed to go to work with anyone else or there would be hell to pay. But if I walk the straight and narrow I'm free of it all.

I begin going to sweat lodge on Sunday nights.

God has many faces and names. Many paths. My way is a thousand fold and one. Tunkashela. The Great Spirit.

The morning I get out of treatment there is a huge spider and web on the steering wheel of my truck. My rent is late and I was evicted. The utility companies are sending disconnection notices. My phone is shut off. I don't have any money. I don't have any food. I have a cold. I feel restless.

Everything is going to be fine.

Within a few days I begin practicing Asana yoga again, move into a new apartment, and find a new job working general labor for a small construction company.

I have trouble adjusting to this new life. Not always sure what to do with my free time.

I go to a thrift store to buy some pants. In the corner of my eye I catch *The Lady of Shallot*. The same magnificent painting that hung over my fireplace all during the Babalon Isis Working. I buy this one since I don't have the old one.

Last night I dreamed I was in a rocky place, like a cave behind waterfalls. Hillary was there. I uncovered an endless black hole. I asked Hillary to help me close it. She wouldn't. She left me. It was the Abyss.

Thy will be done. Not mine.

I begin doing the LBRP again before and after my regular Asana meditation.

I have trouble falling asleep at night without either journaling or my Asana.

A new moon and a solar eclipse.

I have to check myself into jail. Sucks that I'll be in jail for Halloween, but at least it's work release and detectives have backed off of me, realizing I am legit now.

I have a dream about Soror Babalon. We were talking on the phone, but we were sitting on her bed just a few feet away from each other. I finally kiss her. We talk a bit more and then make out. She sucks in her gut as I rub her stomach. A vivid dream.

I take a shower at the witching hour to cleanse my body for a ritual. Perform the LBRP. Asana nude. I see images of a male elf collecting gold in a floating arch. He has a book he is teaching me from, but I sense he is not trustworthy.

Babalon comes to me. She complains of sensing Babalon. Feeling possessed at times. She's been drinking a lot, but nothing else. But she has been drinking every day.

I ask her what she wants me to do. I tell her I don't mess around with magick anymore.

She says, "Please, help me banish her. Help me exorcize her."

"Okay, what do you suggest?"

"You're the magician." She rolls her eyes. "What do you think? It has to be sex magick to be strong enough to work against the Babalon Isis Working. I know that."

"Okay. It's your obsession. You decide what you want to do. I'll help you. You know that. I'm a bit shocked to see you. I thought you hated me."

"I do hate you. I hate you very much." She grinds her teeth. "I fucking hate you," she growls in a harsh whisper. "You broke my heart and I will never forgive that."

I take a step back, feeling shame. "You broke my heart."

"It doesn't matter." She holds both hands up. "Do this for me. You owe me."

"I said I will."

"Alright. This Saturday for Saturn and Binah." Her voice steadily calms as she talks. She was in our bastard order. Our ronin order. She was Soror Babalon. At our peak we reached forty-seven initiates. A secret society in the truest sense. The only member of our bastard order that I talk to any more is Spartan. I don't even know how to find any of the rest. I might be able to track down a few, but have no reason to. And some of them wouldn't even want to talk to me. Some of them would.

"I can do it Saturday."

"You write the ritual up. I'll bring a sigil of Babalon. To destroy during gnosis."

"Why do you want to do this with me?"

"Because we started it together. We did it. I know we can end it."

I nod. "What time?"

"We start at seven pm. I've thought about this for awhile now. I know what I'm doing. I'm doing this one last work with you, Natas, then I'm never touching magick again. Never speaking the name of Babalon. It's evil. And I'm never going to speak to you again. I don't want to remember you."

"Okay," I nod quietly. "I'll see you Saturday then."

"I have robes," she says as she walks toward the door to leave. "You need to make the altar and tools, if you don't have them already."

"Alright. I'll see you Saturday."

She leaves. I sit there thinking about all this. I have to admit the thought of sex with Babalon again is appealing. It's Monday. I can get things ready. She's right about everything. The working drove us both batty. She trusted me. I didn't know how to cope with warping reality affecting us psychologically. That's all magick is. Very advanced psychology.

———⋆———

Saturday evening. It's spring. The leaves outside are just beginning to bud with green. The last of the snow melted away weeks ago.

Soror Babalon sits on my bed with me. We both wear black robes and nothing else. The lights are off. In the center of the room is a black double-cubed altar. Really two wooden boxes I painted black. Atop the altar sits a simple glass cup, a wooden wand, a wooden disk painted with a pentacle, and a small knife. On a small violet and gold cloth before the altar are Tarot cards—the Knight of Swords, the Chariot and Lust—are laid out with burning incense and candles. A small acrylic painting—a woman with green skin, red hair, and a vagina in her forehead—sits among the other magickal tools. Babalon painted the image of Babalon. My magickal diary is next to the painting, open to a blank page.

We are both freshly bathed. Our foreheads are anointed in oil, marking us priest king and priestess queen. The Mark of the Beast and Babylon.

Both of us are barefoot on the carpet.

Soror Babalon knocks on the altar once.

I say, "I Parsifal declare this Temple of the Babalon Isis Lodge of the Poor Bastard Order of Ronin Illuminati open."

Soror Babalon knocks on the altar three times.

I pick up the cup from the altar, stand at the east of the altar facing west, dip my fingertips in the water and sprinkle it eastward with a single flick of my hand. "In the name of Shaddai El Chai I purify this Temple in the East." I move to the north with the cup and sprinkle the water. "In the name of Adonai ha Eretz I purify this Temple in the North." And again in the name of Elohim Tzabaoth in the West and Yahweh Tzabaoth in the South. I return the cup to the altar.

Soror Babalon picks up a burning stick of incense from the small cloth on the floor. She stands at the east of the altar, facing west. Holding the smoking incense in her right hand she draws a pentagram in the air before her saying, "I consecrate with fire in the name of Enlil." She does the same for north, west, and south—Pan, Poseidon and Horus respectively. She returns the incense to its holder on the cloth.

Circumambulation. We raise the astral light by walking around the temple at a brisk pace, clockwise, visualizing the light of the ALL stretching to us, wider, brighter, stronger. Three times we circle.

Together we pray, "Holy art Thou, Lord of the Universe. Holy art Thou, Whom Nature hath not Formed. Holy art Thou the Vast and Mighty One. Lord of the Light and of the Darkness." We both place a shushing index finger to the top lip and whisper, "Twenty-two silence for the Great Work."

At this point we both take a moment to say a private, silent prayer.

We begin with the Lesser Banishment Ritual of the Pentagram (banishing all evil and unwanted spirits) followed by the Middle Pillar Ritual (balancing us and strengthening our connection to the astral light). This is followed by the Banishment Ritual of the Hexagram.

And we begin the main working.

Babalon and I stand before each other on the bed, on our knees in the candlelight. Our eyes locked. We simply stare at each and breathe for some time. Relaxing. We've done this many times before. We pull our robes over our heads, naked before one another.

We go through the motions. A little of everything to build up our sexual energy. To stimulate. Licking. Kissing.

She mounts me with the painting in her hand and whispers, "I am Babalon the whore and great mother."

Sitting atop me and stroking me while I mumble, "I am Horus your lover."

I watch her breasts jiggle as she strokes her nipples. It excites me.

"Don't come in me," she orders.

I nod, fondling her breasts and she guides me into her.

I stare at her beauty and imagine her as the goddess Babalon and I am Horus. The longer we have sex and pick up rhythm, building toward climax, the more real the imagining seems to become. I know Babalon is visualizing something similar to me. We are in our own world. A globe of candle light in the astral plane.

Time is lost to us. I gaze at the wand working with the grail mesmerized. There is nothing but the sound of our heavy breathing and tiny moans. At some point Babalon pants, "We have to cum together. Banish her as we cum."

"I know."

"Are you ready?"

It takes me a moment to answer. "Yes."

She begins to moan frantically. The moan begins to sound like she is singing. Singing in Hebrew and Latin. I listen to the tongues of an angel. She whimpers, "Oh god, baby, don't stop. Oh god." She begins to squeal and scream. Moving faster. Sloppier. We both take the painting in our hands and rip it in half and we cum and she screams.

Barely catching our breath, we quickly burn each half of the painting with the candles.

She dresses, thanks me, says good-bye, and leaves.

I record the events in my journal as I smoke a cigarette, then go to bed, exhausted.

Back in a bun, her thick, black hair has a healthy shine, making her look alluringly younger than she is. It's a hot summer day. Early afternoon. The sun is high and the sky a tranquil blue. She's tan, naturally tan but more so from the summer sun. Her face is red from exertion and she glistens with sweat in a Halloween orange tank top and white shorts. Her arms and legs are toned. Her stomach flat. Her chest busty and firm, respectfully embraced with a modest bra.

She leans in the doorway with her hand resting on one side of the frame and the shoulder pressed against the other. She bends forward just a tad, a large blotch of sweat on the front of her orange shirt making a Rorschach design up her waist and stomach between her breasts.

She catches her breath and gazes for a long at me before she speaks. "May I have some water, Natas?"

My mouth is open is utter surprise. I shake my head at the sound of her voice. "Yes. Of course. I'm just shocked to see you, Soror Lucid. Come in."

She follows me into my new home and into the kitchen. I get her some water. "All I have is tap."

"That's fine," Lucid nods, beads of cooling sweat on her forehead, dripping down her arms. Tiny beads speckled on her nose and upper lip.

She takes several large gulps, and catches her breath as the glass leaves her lips. "Oh, that's good."

"The water of life," I mumble. "I'm surprised to see you. I thought I'd been shunned."

"You have." She bluntly states, taking a sip of water.

"So what are you doing here?"

"A few reasons. It's true you created quite a scandal in our little secret world. Made a laughingstock of yourself. Made it into *Liber Nutz*. I heard rumors about you being strung out on drugs. Then I'd see you on the news." She shakes her head. I give an embarrassed smile. "Getting arrested for everything from assault and disorderly conduct to selling drugs and stealing."

"Yeah, I kind of spun out of control there for a minute," I continued with a meek smile.

"Is this clean? Can I use this?" She holds up a white dish towel from my kitchen counter.

I nod. "It's clean."

She wipes her forehead and dabs the sweat off her face. "I heard that you joined other groups. I heard that you attempted to cross the Abyss. Took the Oath of the Abyss and went crazy. Tried to start your own order."

"A lot of weird, bad shit happened. How did you hear all this?"

She sighs. "Azazel and Alpha."

"Oh."

"I talked to Frater Spartan, too."

"Really? How did you meet him?"

"Alpha told me to ask him about you, said you'd been working with him and some others in your order. When I talked to him, he'd told me your order took off fast and fell apart faster. He said once you vanished the rest dropped like flies. He was an interesting fellow."

I smile. "I guess you didn't give up on me."

"No, I didn't." She shakes her head, shyly looking down at the ground. "I got a divorce."

"Wow."

"I still have your poems from when you were in the order."

"Wow, those are old. Years ago. I'm embarrassed to have written them."

"You shouldn't be."

I shrug.

Her cheeks are not as flushed as they were before she drank the water. "I left the order about a year after you did."

"Huh. Yeah, I left all my orders except one. So you've given magick up?"

"No." Her brown eyes and thick lashes. "That's why I'm here."

I raise my eyebrows and look at the floor.

She continues. "While I was in the Akashic, the angel Raziel spoke to me. He said you have knowledge and seek knowledge not meant for humans. I asked him what could be done. He told me you need to make sure you do things in order. He said you need to redeem yourself."

"I haven't practiced much magick lately. I'm a bit rusty. Half afraid to get so deep into it again. That's cool that you're still practicing. What have you been doing? Are you working with anyone?"

"I'm not working with anyone. I've been doing it on my own. I've found what I need. I don't need the politics of the group any more."

"I still can't resist sigil work. A little Asana and LBRPs. Nothing much else. Really, I find myself entering states of gnosis without realizing it until its happened. I can't stop the lucid dreaming either. I have to keep tunnel vision to avoid sighting omens. I don't think about the future. I just float. Lost. I try not to think about numbers or space and time. Or God. I've just recently started reading again. I'm sorry. I'm babbling." I think of Babalon at the sound of that last word.

"It's okay." Lucid smiles at me, her brown eyes bright and warm. "I've been meditating. I guess I think of myself as a shaman now. I astral travel. Work with the Zodiac.

Been exploring the magick of my ancestors. Gypsies. But mostly I've been exploring shamanism and growing herbs and plants. I read a lot of poetry. I got a new job, too."

"Doing what?"

"Working in a greenhouse."

"Wow. Very cool."

"Yeah, I'm a tree hugger now."

"So why are you here again?"

"That sounds so welcoming."

"That's not the way I meant to say it. I'm just surprised is all. It's been what? Five or six years?"

"Over six," she nods. "Can we sit down?"

"Yes. Of course." I lead her into the living room and the couch. "How did you get here?"

"I jogged."

"Uh huh," I nod. "And how did you know where I live?"

"Frater Spartan said he talked to Soror Zoso."

"Ah," the light bulb blinks on in my head.

"What's the story with Zoso?"

I shrug. "Not much. She was in my order with Spartan. She's helping me privately publish some things under an alias. Editing and such."

"Spartan and Alpha said they've been reading it. I've been reading it."

I nod, press my knuckle against my lower lip. Her legs still look damp from sweating. Her shirt is drying but still visibly moist. She is close enough that I can smell her sweat. I enjoy the scent.

Her bare knee accidently touches mine. Her skin is smooth and cool now. Lightly sticky from her drying sweat. Her eyes look at me the instant our flesh connects. She blurts out, "I want to work with you."

"What do you mean?"
"I want to help you out of the dark night."

"Adventure? Excitement? A Jedi craves not these things."
— Yoda, *Star Wars, Episode V, The Empire Strikes Back*

After a few weeks of working with Soror Lucid I begin to analyze my magickal journals from the Babalon Isis Working (still amazed at the change in handwriting styles throughout the Working) in an attempt to uncover the root of my stumbling into the Abyss. We bury ourselves in Gematria. Here is an entry that set off alarms. I was excited. Brash. Naïve.

It was confusing. At first I thought it was the wrong entity. Realization was that Hermes-Thoth was invoked in many forms. Should stick to one form in the future. Discussed some issues. The jealousy of angels. Aliens are real. I am God. Union with God. All is God. Secret Chiefs? "They're not ready for you."

Originally the entity tried to intimidate and was very playful, tricky, lying, testing.

I exerted control over the situation with the thought of will to power and stating many of my names.

At this point Hermes-Thoth acknowledged me. This is when he explained that I summoned him in too many forms.

Hadit was also there/possibly was entity Hermes-Thoth.

On the right path. Asked for success in magick. Recommended I keep my job and pass my testing. Said my current project will be published.

There seemed to be tiny fluttering and dancing elf-like entities. Enormous glob behind me/Hermes in too many forms.

The thought that it might be the wrong entity, a gut feeling that should have been investigated. The entity did explain that the reason it came in multiple forms was because I used multiple and diverse images to summon it. More likely the multiple forms were multiple entities.

The entity was intimidating, tricky, lying and testing? All signs of a negative entity.

The sense of the presence of Hadit is also a warning sign. Hadit is Set, who betrays and kills his twin brother Osiris. This was Set who appeared, not Hermes-Thoth.

Again, Hermes in too many forms, an enormous glob, tiny fluttering and dancing elf-like entities. In my excitement to succeed and move forward, I overlooked all of this.

More diary entries of Invocations of this same entity I spoke with initially:

Invoke Hermes-Thoth
Hermes-Thoth came through mist this time. Much more clear. Told me to write the Book of **********. Much more friendly this time. Said he will help me.

Invoke Hermes-Thoth
Discussion, love making, some sigils have worked. Study knowledge lectures, prepare to become Zelator. Write. Continue daily workings as permitted. Past lives are "true". Floating cross legged, made out with me, fondled, laid with me, warned to be careful with sigils. Write Invocation of Hermes-Thoth. No black magick.

Invoke Hermes-Thoth

Reading of the Emerald Tablet
Hermes instructed me in breathing and meditation techniques. Reached moment in meditation that was the same or a similar state of consciousness to that of my birth memory. The stillness of mind/blackness/non-thought. Said I am Galabram. Said I'm not prepared to understand tablet.

Amazingly, a few months later, in the beginning of the Bablon Isis Working I receive a strange and random message from Tahuti (during a ritual divination) attempting to communicate a mistake I'd made. This was the angelic Tahuti, an aspect of the Hermes-Thoth I originally attempted to invoke. I was confused by the apparent disturbance in my work by this Tahuti and ignored it, making only a minor note of it.

Soror Lucid and I sit together drinking tea at her coffee table discussing my current work. I've agreed to daily LBRPs and nothing else while we sort things out. When we work together in ritual we spend a lot of time in Tiphareth and the Middle Pillar. Right now we are examining another journal entry of mine.

I admit a total loss of direction at the onset of the Black Odyssey. I sit here confused and bumbling, attempting to make sense of it all and feeling no direction. Now the goal is to learn to behave like a gentleman.

"What do you think it means 'to behave like a gentleman,'" she asks.

"To be virtuous. To live by a code. Like the strict oaths of the old mystery schools when divine magick was practiced rather than simple sorcery like chaos magick."

"Maybe." She gives me and affectionate smile, a teacher proud of a learning student. "How do you feel about things now?"

"Really, I'm fine. I feel like I'm back on track. Feeling confident and humble. I've put away my Thoth deck. I'm using the Waite deck right now, until I make my own."

Lucid nods. "Always remember you have spiritual rights. There is a goodness hidden in the center. I think you're alright now, too." She looks away from me. "I'm going to be leaving now. I'm moving back to Germany."

"Oh." I'm surprised, sad. "That's cool. I'll miss you."

"We'll stay in touch." She takes my hand in hers and smiles at me.

"Maybe I'll visit you some day."

"That would be nice."

"Thank you for helping me, Lucid."

"You're welcome."

At lunch break one afternoon, sitting in my hardhat, I catch a newspaper article about a big drug bust including Luba and Clint. Luba was sentenced to four years in prison. Clint ten.

Yesterday I ran into Martin Two Eagles downtown. He's homeless now. He told me Texas was robbed while I was in rehab and nearly beaten to death.

I'm empathetic, and grateful to have escaped their fates.

That night I perform the LBRP, feeling serene. I follow up with the Middle Pillar and a Tarot reading. I pray and wonder.

There are two original fountains of magick. The first source was given to Adam and the House of David by messengers of God. The second source was given to humans by the fallen, rebel angels. My initiations came through personal study and work, and the tutelage of fallen angels.

During the Odyssey I learned of secret societies of another sort. Secret societies of criminals. People like any other. Hidden societies exist in many forms, from the self-help group to the criminal/drug addict network, to the Masonic and esoteric. I know this is true. I have experienced it.

Looking at words in my magickal diary: *45 days in jail, paperwork error, 45 = Galahad*

She licked my forehead. My third I opened.
Osiris died and was born again as Horus.
Sophos. Nous. Logos.
The animal soul under will.
I am an initiate.
There is the serpent's apple.
There is Ahra-Mazda and Ahriman.
And there is ALL.

About the Author

Nathan Neuharth is a writer and artist. He is currently the editor of *kult ov kaos* magazine. He has eight years experience in the mental health field and is a former chemical dependency counselor with degrees in Liberal Arts and Human Services. Nathan has been experimenting with shamanism and ritual magick since 1989.